MW00880993

SLEEPING WITH A NARCISSIST

PSYCHOLOGOCAL INSIGHTS INTO THE WORLD OF NARCISSISTIC PERSONALITY DISORDER

THIS BOOK IS UNVEILING MANIPULATIVE TACTICS AND EQUIPPING YOU WITH TOOLS TO PROTECT YOUR MENTAL AND EMOTIONAL HEALTH

LIUBOV GULBRANDSEN

DISCLOSURE

This book is designed to provide information that the author believes to be accurate regarding the subject matter discussed. No warranty is made concerning the accuracy or completeness of the information contained herein. Both the author and the publisher specifically disclaim any responsibility for any liability, loss, or risk, personal or otherwise, that may result directly or indirectly from the use and application of any of the contents of this book.

Furthermore, this book is not intended to serve as the basis for any personal decision. It should not be interpreted as a recommendation for specific actions, or advice. Each case is individual. Readers are encouraged to seek professional guidance tailored to their unique situations.

The author incorporates examples of real stories from real people; however, many names and identifying characteristics have been changed to protect their privacy. The narratives included are illustrative and should not be construed as endorsements or guarantees of any particular outcome.

By reading this book, you acknowledge and accept that the information provided is for informational purposes only and that you assume full responsibility for any actions taken based on the content herein.

CONTENTS

PREFACE

Countless individuals grapple with the difficulty of being in a relationship with a narcissist. It deeply pains me to witness these situations, yet I believe I have discovered a path forward. The key lies in understanding the individual you are involved with.

Knowledge is indeed power, and recognizing the manipulative tactics of narcissists empowers you to assert yourself and stand your ground. To illustrate the profound harm and suffering caused by narcissists, I have compiled a few stories from their partners, as well as - in solidarity - support and advice offered by others.

HOW DO YOU LEAVE?

Claire: *"How do you leave? Like it shouldn't be hard for me, I don't live with him, and I don't have kids with him. It's been three years of on and off and times of pure hell and other times the best times I've had in my life. I know I need to leave, and I know we're not good for each other. I know that I* *would not reintroduce him to my children and family again. I just feel like without him I have no one, I have no friends nothing and always end up going back. Please help me I am pathetic…"*

Beth: *"You aren't pathetic. A lot of us have dealt with narcs. They are just professionals at getting us to think that things will get better with them, but it never does. You should watch videos on how being with a narc affects our overall health. Narcs know how keep us confused (should I stay or go, did that really just happen or am I crazy, he'll change or will he, this hurts but there are good times, so I'll stay, etc.) This pertains to both genders.*

I hope you leave. Trust me. You WILL have friends, family and new people will continue to come into your life as long as you live! I stopped giving my "ex" the right to treat me, however. I couldn't take the disrespect, lies, insults and being used. Best decision ever. I was only with him for 7 months. Now, I'm off dating apps and listening to videos on how to heal with a narc, how to avoid or break up with one and the minds of a narc. You deserve to be with someone that won't make you feel like this."

Brian: *"You are not pathetic. Most likely trauma bonded. In bad times our brains are programmed to hang onto the good times. This is an intentional manipulation technique used by the narcissist. Build you up then knock you down. And the pattern repeats. Someone once gave me a great piece of advice. Sending hugs."*

Allisson: *"You are very lucky that you don't have kids with him. Get out before you do, otherwise you will be stuck dealing with his abuse for the rest of your life. But I do understand how you feel. Before I got pregnant, which was unintentional, I knew I needed to leave but couldn't. They set it up this way from the beginning, all the manipulations and lies. It makes it almost impossible to leave."*

WHEN DOES IT GET BETTER?

Emme: *"I've been in no contact for exactly 4 months tomorrow. I was doing good, and it feels like in the past month, I've lost it. I'm not strong enough. I am in mental turmoil. Missing him, ruminating. I'm failing at life because of it… it makes me introverted at my job. I have a seven-year-old daughter and I feel like I'm never fully present with her or giving enough. I try not to, but I've broken down in front of her. My entire house is a mess… I already have adhd, so it's hard…and I try to force myself to organize, but depression from when I was with him, and now, after him, has taken its toll. I feel like I live on top of piles, and I CAN'T get in a place mentally where I can tackle it. I feel like I can't fix anything, and I'm trapped. Completely trapped. and I will just sit here in a hoarder house, paralyzed, and die… When does it get better?"*

Susan: *"I'm sorry to hear that you're going through such a tough time right now. It's completely understandable to feel overwhelmed and trapped, especially after going through a breakup and dealing with depression. Remember that you're not alone, and there are ways to gradually work towards feeling better.*

Firstly, it's important to be kind to yourself and acknowledge that healing takes time. Recovery is a process, and it's normal to have ups and downs along the way. It's okay to have moments of weakness, as long as you keep trying to move forward.

To start, try breaking down your tasks into smaller, more manageable steps. Focus on one area of your house at a time and set small goals for each day. It might be helpful to create a schedule or a to-do list to keep track of your progress. Celebrate even the smallest accomplishments, as they can help boost your motivation.

When it comes to organizing, consider seeking support from friends or family members who may be willing to help you. Sometimes having someone alongside you can make the process feel less overwhelming. Additionally, therapy or counseling could be beneficial in addressing your depression and providing guidance during this challenging time.

Remember, taking care of yourself is essential to be there for your daughter. Although it may be difficult, try to find moments throughout the day where you can fully engage with her. It could be something as simple as reading a book together or playing a game. Quality time doesn't always have to be extravagant; it's the connection and presence that truly matter.

Lastly, know that it does get better with time and effort. Healing is a personal journey, and everyone's timeline is different. Surround yourself with positive influences, seek support from loved ones, and be patient with yourself. You have already shown strength by reaching out for help. Keep moving forward, one step at a time, and you will find yourself in a better place eventually."

Anna: *It sounds like you may need counseling and getting out and about. Go places with your daughter and meet other parents. Make a fresh/ healthy life. You deserve better than the aftermath of a narcissist!!*

HAS ANYONE EVER FOUND SUCCESS WITH A NARCISSIST?

Campbell: *"Hello, I am writing for honest help and no criticism. I don't need the negativity. I am 25 and in a relationship with a narcissist. I was going to leave him and was in the process until I found out I was pregnant. I chose to stay because I fear the potential hell he would take me through trying to take my baby. I also can't imagine allowing him time alone away from me with the baby. He has agreed to couples' therapy. Has anyone ever found any success with their narcissist? I'd rather live in hell and know my baby is safe than leave him with the potential to hurt my baby. I'm just hoping there is a light at the end and possibility of change. Thank you".*

Beth: *"Staying won't make your baby safe, it will expose them to abuse. Even if your partner treats them like gold (though the odds of that are slim), your child will witness your degradation and the abuse that happens to you.*

They will witness you walking in eggs shells and grow up with the same habits. They will see your nervous system be shot and either feel responsible (because they are a kid) or think it's ok to treat someone the way you are being treated.

We think we can shield them and withstand the storm, but it damages them in ways we can't see until the damage is done. Please get out now. The older you kid gets, the harder it is.

As far as counseling goes, it all depends. But you don't need to be in the firing line during the processes until he figures it out."

Megan: *"He's not going to change I'm not going to tell you to leave because you have to decide that on your own, but that baby will witness everything that goes on. You can always fight to have his visits supervised and monitored etc. when and if you decide to leave. Leaving early on would ensure that child has at least one stable happy home to be in."*

———

"Sleeping With a Narcissist" is more than just a book—it's a vital tool for anyone entangled in or recovering from a relationship with a narcissist. It provides the knowledge and strategies necessary to move from survival to thriving, embodying the resilience of the human spirit. By immersing yourself in its material, reflecting on your experiences, and implementing its strategies, you embark on a transformative journey toward healing and growth. As you progress through each page, remember that you are not alone, and armed with knowledge and tools, you can transition from mere survival to thriving.

So let us embark on this journey together with open hearts and minds, poised for healing and growth.

INTRODUCTION

Today, millions find themselves entangled in emotionally disorientating, manipulative, and deeply damaging relationships where one partner exhibits the defining traits of narcissism while the other feels isolated and misunderstood, questioning his or her reality.

Narcissistic abuse, as a form of emotional abuse, affects the victims' minds; hence, other people cannot see it. However, it has a much deeper and harmful effect on victims' health and lives than any physical abuse...

"Sleeping With a Narcissist" is not merely a recount of personal experiences. It is a structured guide designed to educate and empower you - the reader - whether you are currently in the grips of a narcissistic relationship, survived one, or are a keen learner of psychological behaviors and personal development. Through these pages, I aim to provide valuable insights into narcissistic traits, their psychological effects on victims, and practical strategies for dealing with narcissistic individuals.

You, the reader, are my main concern. Narcissists tend to choose partners who they see as a reflection of themselves or who can boost their self-esteem. They look for individuals who are empathetic, nurturing, and willing to cater to their needs without expecting much in return. Narcissists often seek out people who are willing to admire and praise them constantly, as this feeds their ego. They choose individuals who, they believe, are easily manipulated, partners who will prioritize their needs above their own, allowing the narcissist to maintain a sense of power and control in the relationship.

Successful individuals can be particularly vulnerable to narcissists because their achievements and status may make them an attractive target for someone seeking to boost their self-esteem or image. Narcissists may be drawn to successful individuals because they see them as a means to elevate their social standing or gain access to resources and opportunities. Additionally, successful people may be more likely to overlook warning signs of narcissistic behavior due to their busy schedules or desire to maintain a positive public image.

Initially, narcissists may admire certain qualities in their partners, such as kindness, generosity, or success, as these traits reflect positively on the narcissist. However, as the relationship progresses, the narcissist may start to feel threatened by these same qualities, perceiving them as a challenge to their sense of superiority. In turn, they may begin to belittle, criticize, or blame their partner for possessing these qualities, using them as a means to undermine the partner's self-esteem and maintain control of the relationship. This behavior can create a cycle of praise followed by blame, where the narcissist alternates between idealizing and devaluing their partner to maintain power and dominance.

As the relationship continues, narcissists may become increasingly critical of their partner's positive qualities, viewing them as threats to their self-image. They may try to diminish their partners' accomplishments, talents, or strengths to assert their superiority and maintain control. This behavior can be emotionally manipulative and damage the partner's self-esteem, leading to feelings of confusion, self-doubt, and inadequacy. In essence, the narcissist's initial admiration for their partner's qualities may transform into a source of resentment and blame as they seek to maintain their sense of power and dominance in the relationship.

Narcissists seek out partners who are willing to overlook their "faults and mistakes," creating an environment where the narcissists' behaviors are constantly validated and reinforced. Such partners are often highly empathetic and forgiving, more likely to tolerate narcissists' selfish and manipulative tendencies. Overall, narcissists look for partners who will enable their behavior and provide them with the admiration and attention they crave.

Before engaging in relationships, narcissists will test their victims to gauge their vulnerability. Initially, they shower the victim with excessive praise, attention, and affection to see how responsive and easily influenced they are. Subsequently, they will try ignoring or withdrawing their affection to see whether their victims will try to please them to regain their approval.

Narcissists will constantly test the boundaries by pushing their victims to see how much control they can exert over them without resistance. These manipulations allow the narcissist to assess the victim's emotional vulnerabilities, willingness to comply, and susceptibility to manipulation, enabling them to exploit these weaknesses for their benefit.

Some people may not be suitable targets or victims for narcissists due to various factors, such as strong boundaries, self-confidence, and a healthy sense of self-worth. Individuals who are assertive, independent, and able to recognize manipulative behavior are less likely to fall prey to narcissists' tactics. Additionally, those who prioritize their well-being, maintain healthy relationships, and set clear boundaries are less appealing to narcissists who thrive on control and power dynamics. Ultimately, people who value themselves, trust their instincts, and prioritize their happiness are less likely to be manipulated or exploited.

It can be extremely difficult to engage in a relationship with a narcissist due to their maladaptive behaviors that are often manipulative and confusing to partners. Spouses who fall for narcissists are often people-pleasing types who go the extra mile to keep their partner happy. They want the best for their partner, and the narcissist capitalizes on this type of person.

This book was crafted for those of you who are navigating the turbulent waters of a current relationship, healing from past abuse, or intrigued by the complexities of human behavior. It is structured to not only inform but also support and empower you through knowledge and shared experiences.

As a member of various esteemed women's associations in the United States, I have dedicated years to studying the nuances of narcissistic abuse. My commitment extends beyond personal interest to foster a community of informed, resilient individuals who can advocate for themselves and others in the face of psychological adversity.

This book unfolds over several chapters designed to help you better understand narcissism, identify its manifestations in relationships, and equip you with coping and healing strategies. From the initial signs of narcissistic behavior to the complex journey of recovery, the content is structured to provide clarity and support at every stage.

The road to recovery from narcissistic abuse is undoubtedly challenging, but it is also a journey of profound transformation and empowerment. As you turn each page, remember that you are not alone, and with the right tools and understanding, you can move from surviving to thriving.

I invite you to engage deeply with the material presented, reflect on your experiences, and apply the strategies outlined. This book is more than just a read; it is a step toward healing and a testament to the strength of the human spirit in the face of adversity. Let us begin this journey together with open hearts and minds, ready to heal and grow.

CHAPTER 1
UNMASKING THE NARCISSIST

I n a society that often celebrates charm and confidence, it can be alarmingly easy to overlook the sinister undercurrents that define a narcissist. The term itself is flung around casually, often misused to label anyone who seems self-centered or boastful. However, true narcissistic personality disorder (NPD) is a serious psychological condition that can wreak havoc on relationships, leaving emotional devastation in its wake. This chapter peels back the layers of narcissism, starting from its deep-seated psychological origins to the subtle signs. Understanding these elements is crucial for anyone standing in the shadow of a narcissist, as they provide the knowledge needed to recognize, navigate, and ultimately protect oneself from the long-term damage these individuals can cause.

1.1 THE PSYCHOLOGY OF NARCISSISM: ROOTS AND RECOGNITION

The journey into the psychology of narcissism began over a century ago with its first conceptualization by Sigmund Freud. Freud introduced the world to the idea of narcissism as a normal stage in the human developmental process characterized by self-love and the drive toward personal perfection. However, when these characteristics become overly magnified, they metamorphose into what today's psychologists recognize as NPD. It is important to distinguish people with NPD, which is a diagnosable mental health condition, from those who exhibit narcissistic behavior.

NPD is a set of personality traits characterized by a grandiose sense of self, self-centeredness, arrogant presentation, an excessive need for attention and admiration, and a lack of empathy. Individuals with NPD typically display these traits across a range of situations and over a long period. These people have a broken emotional core; they struggle with experiencing and expressing emotions like love and empathy in a typical or healthy manner. People with NPD may have challenges forming deep, meaningful connections with others, including romantic partners. Their love may be perceived as shallow, conditional on receiving admiration or validation, or driven by self-serving motives, which significantly affects their relationships, work, and overall functioning. NPD diagnosis should be done by mental health professionals who assess individuals based on specific criteria and symptoms.

People who exhibit narcissistic behavior may not meet the full criteria for NPD or have it as a diagnosable disorder. Their behaviors might be situational, temporary, or less extreme compared to individuals with NPD.

The severity, persistence, and clinical diagnosis differentiate Narcissistic Personality Disorder from the more general concept of narcissistic behavior.

Despite outward displays of confidence and grandiosity, individuals with NPD often have deep-seated feelings of inadequacy or insecurity. Their behaviors and attitudes serve as a defense mechanism to protect them against these underlying vulnerabilities.

Narcissists can come from varied family backgrounds, but some common patterns may contribute to the development of narcissistic traits. In some cases, narcissists may have grown up in families where there was an emphasis on external appearances, achievements, or status, leading them to prioritize their image and success above all else. They may have experienced inconsistent or conditional love, where they felt they had to earn approval and validation through meeting certain expectations or standards set by their caregivers. Additionally, growing up in an environment where emotional needs were neglected or dismissed could also contribute to the development of narcissistic traits, as the individual learns to prioritize their own needs and desires to compensate for feelings of inadequacy or insecurity. Overall, the family environment in which a narcissist grows up plays a role in shaping their behaviors, attitudes, and interpersonal relationships.

Narcissists may also lack healthy boundaries in their family, where their boundaries may not have been respected, leading them to have difficulty respecting the boundaries of others as adults. Additionally, they may have been raised in an environment where manipulation, control, or emotional abuse was present, subsequently developing controlling behavior and learning emotional manipulation. Ultimately, the family dynamics and upbringing of narcissists contribute to the development of their narcissistic traits and behaviors, shaping their interpersonal interactions and relationships in adulthood.

People with NPD generally attribute problems to others and have difficulty considering their role or responsibility across situations. They often exploit or violate the rights of others without feeling guilty. When they hurt someone, they do not feel sorry for the person, unable to sympathize and understand the feelings of others. They do not even understand that they might hurt or offend the other person. Narcissists can say something unpleasant, make a sharp remark, or be tactless, which may hurt you while they will not feel any guilt.

On the contrary, they will blame you and say, "It's your problem, you are too sensitive, you need to work on yourself." These people cannot feel remorse. If you ask them not to do something again, not to say something, or not to interrupt, they will continue to do the same, not because they forget or do it out of habit but simply because they cannot sympathize. This is a clear diagnostic marker: if you ask someone to stop doing something that bothers you, and this individual does not stop, you are likely dealing with a narcissist.

Narcissists tend to belittle those around them to make themselves appear superior. It is especially damaging to kids who find themselves helpless around such people…

Another example would be a date who does not stop talking during the entire date, focusing on him/herself with little consideration for the back-and-forth dialogue between individuals, which would be more socially appropriate.

When you are dating someone with these behaviors, it is not always easy to detect the telltale signs at first because people with narcissistic traits often use charm and flattery to make initial connections before showing their true colors.

The narcissistic person may ask you a few questions about yourself on a first date, but over time, the intrigue will almost always fade, and the focus will return to their own experiences. There is a strong sense of entitlement about prioritizing their own needs.

Narcissists instill feelings of fear, guilt, and inadequacy in their victims to control and manipulate them. A favorite tactic of narcissists is gaslighting, where the victims are made to believe that there is something wrong with their memory and attention and that they are incapable of doing something. We will dedicate a separate chapter to gaslighting. Narcissists always try to extract maximum benefit from a person - material, moral, energetic. Narcissists are energy vampires. Your unpleasant feelings serve as levers of influence for them. To drain your energy, they instill feelings of guilt and shame in you and make you suffer, all while showcasing their perfect image. You become lost, start to submit, and thus fall into their trap. Your suffering and sense of guilt are their source of sustenance.

A history of unstable or short-lived relationships, a tendency to idealize and devalue partners, or a lack of genuine emotional connection leads to difficulties in forming and maintaining healthy, fulfilling connections with others. Narcissists often have a pattern of unstable relationships characterized by frequent breakups, conflicts, and difficulties maintaining long-term connections. This instability may stem from their inability to form deep emotional bonds, prioritize their partner's needs, or sustain healthy communication and conflict resolution skills. They may struggle with intimacy, empathy, and trust, leading to a cycle of idealizing their partners in the beginning stages of a rela-tionship and then devaluing them once their flaws or imperfec-tions become apparent. This pattern of idealization and devaluation can create a sense of emotional chaos and unpre-dictability in their relationships, making it challenging for their partners to feel secure, valued, and respected.

The person with narcissistic traits may initially make attempts to flatter you with compliments or gifts. The positive feedback reinforces the person with narcissistic qualities, and so they continue this pattern for a while. They enjoy being praised but have a difficult time congratulating peers for accomplishments when the reverse situation comes up.

Those who are in a relationship with narcissistic people might be frustrated by the lack of empathy and support. They may feel as though their needs are not recognized or met. Eventually, the cycle becomes tiresome, leading to increased conflict within the relationship.

One of my friends, a victim of a narcissistic husband, was so suppressed and devalued in her relationship that she started to think of herself as mentally unstable. This often happens to victims of narcissism. She decided to share her feelings with her husband and told him: "I feel so bad right now, I even want to end my life. I keep thinking about how to resist suicide." In this statement, there was a plea for help, but for her husband, it was a blow to his ego. He just jumped up in indignation: "Are you saying that I am so bad that you are ready to die just to not live with me? Are you suggesting that I am a failure?" While the victims might be trying to save their lives, their narcissist partners will try to save their self-esteem. The lack of empathy prevents them from understanding how their significant others feel. They do not care about their victims' lives; their main goal is to numb their pain. When communicating with a narcissist, avoid criticism, do not speak about your feelings, and do not open up, as your information will be used against you.

My friend found herself in a very difficult situation, facing aggressive and unempathetic behavior from her narcissistic husband. This is a classic example of how a narcissist reacts to someone's sincere emotions and plea for help - making the situation about themselves and their self-esteem.

If you are in a close relationship, know that a narcissist will never change, and they are not capable of empathy. Criticism, openness, and expression of feelings can be used against you in relationships with a narcissist. Either you agree to feed him with your energy for the rest of your life, or you need to leave.

People with narcissistic personality disorder experience inner emptiness. Their energy is at a very low level. They do not know who they really are, and they constantly doubt themselves; therefore, they need to maintain their self-image through others. They need approval and admiration from others as a source of energy, and that is why we feel drained when communicating with a narcissist. They extract approval energy from us, filling their emptiness. Entering a relationship with a narcissist is dangerous because you can lose everything - energy, emotions, the desire to live.

Narcissistic personality disorder is not diagnosed until adulthood; however, the manifestation of narcissism typically starts during childhood or adolescence. Pathological narcissism is more commonly diagnosed in males due to genetic and environmental factors.

1.2 SUBTLE SIGNS: BEYOND THE OBVIOUS NARCISSISTIC TRAITS

When addressing narcissistic personality disorder, the spotlight often falls on their disruptive behaviors—grandiose self-importance, blatant disregard for others, and overt acts of manipulation. However, beneath these apparent traits lie subtler yet equally damaging tactics that can slowly erode one's sense of self and destabilize foundational relationships. These less overt manipulation tactics, often overshadowed by their more blatant counterparts, require a keen eye and deep understanding to identify and counteract effectively.

Passive-aggressiveness is one such tactic that can be particularly confusing. This behavior often manifests in ways that can initially appear harmless or even normal. For instance, a narcissist might offer a compliment that, upon closer inspection, carries a cutting undertone. Imagine a scenario where, after a work presentation, a narcissist says to their colleague, "You seemed so relaxed during your presentation today; luckily, no one noticed the errors." Here, what masquerades as praise is actually a subtle jab. This backhanded compliment not only sows seeds of doubt in the recipient but also elevates the narcissist by subtly pointing out their keen attention to detail and supposed honesty. Recognizing these double-edged expressions is crucial, as they are designed to unsettle the recipient, making them question their perceptions and worth.

Equally manipulative is the strategic use of emotional withdrawal. Narcissists adeptly use this tactic to gain control over their partners by creating an environment of psychological uncertainty. Emotional withdrawal can be as straightforward as the silent treatment or more nuanced, like sudden disengagement in conversations or the withholding of affection. For example, consider a situation where a partner discusses plans for a future vacation, and the narcissist, feeling neither the center of attention nor in control of the plans, suddenly becomes cold and distant. This shift is often so subtle and unexpected that it leaves the partner feeling destabilized and anxious, eager to restore harmony by any means necessary, often by ceding more control to the narcissist.

Victimhood and martyrdom are roles that narcissists often assume with great effect. By portraying themselves as perpetual victims, they seek not only to garner sympathy but also to manipulate those around them. This behavior can frequently be observed in scenarios where accountability is demanded. For instance, if a narcissist is confronted about neglecting responsibilities at home, they might respond with an exaggerated recounting of their work stress and health issues, framing these as reasons why they should not be held accountable for household duties. This tactic diverts attention from their failings and elicits sympathy and support, often resulting in the partner taking on more than their fair share of responsibilities, further entrenching the narcissist's control.

The inconsistency in a narcissist's behavior adds a layer of complexity to their manipulation. This unpredictability can range from mood swings and unpredictable responses to commitments to sudden changes in plans or preferences. Such inconsistencies are often strategically employed to keep partners off-balance. For example, a narcissist may express enthusiasm for a partner's new job opportunity, only to later dismiss it as unimportant or not worth discussing. This kind of behavioral unpredictability creates a dynamic where the partner feels constantly on edge, unable to predict or understand what will trigger negative responses or disapproval from the narcissist.

Lastly, narcissists suffer from poisonous envy. A narcissist envies others deep down, but on the exterior, they attempt to make it appear as though they are the ones to be envied. They cannot sleep peacefully when someone is doing very well, but they are very happy about someone else's misfortune. A narcissist literally feels bad if you are doing well. They need to do everything to make you feel bad, too. For example, if you have achieved something, rejoice in it, and want to share your joy, this person may belittle you and diminish your achievement. They will do every-thing to make you feel like you have not really achieved anything special. In general, you feel a strong loss of energy. For example, when you want to happily share that you have learned to drive a car, they may say, "Even a bear can learn to ride a bicycle." Alternatively, when you are proud that you have five children, the narcissist will tell you, "You are breeding like a gypsy camp. Having five children does not require much intelligence." Why do they do this? Out of envy, they need to diminish your signifi-cance to feel more significant themselves, and they need to assert themselves at the expense of others.

The most important thing for them is not to lose the feeling of "I am better than everyone else. I am perfection itself," they need to maintain their ideal image in their own eyes. Another cunning move of a narcissist is to attribute your merits to themselves. For example, "Did you get an A? That is because I helped you, not because you are so smart."

There is another characteristic sign of a narcissist. If someone has a misfortune or an unpleasant situation - for example, the power went out, and people are sitting in the dark, or someone got fired - you will see an involuntary smile on the face of a narcissist. Other people's suffering makes them feel good, and they will be in high spirits all evening.

These subtler signs are often overlooked or misinterpreted by those who suffer from them, making them particularly insidious and harmful. Understanding these tactics is essential for anyone involved with a narcissist, as it arms them with the knowledge needed to recognize manipulation in its less obvious forms and to take steps to protect their mental and emotional well-being.

"So, let me get it straight, it's ok for you to be a lying, cheating, manipulating, abusive asshole, but I am the bad one for pointing it out?"

MARIA CONSIGLIO

1.3 THE NARCISSIST'S TOOLBOX

Gaslighting Decoded: Identifying and Combating Psychological Manipulation

Gaslighting is a form of psychological manipulation that seeks to sow seeds of doubt in a targeted individual or members of a group, making them question their memory, perception, or sanity. The term originates from the 1938 stage play "Gas Light," where a husband manipulates his wife into believing she is losing her grip on reality as part of a sinister agenda. A criminal bigamist marries a wealthy young woman to gain control of all her inheritance. To achieve this, he decides to drive her insane. He dims the gas lamps in the house, making the light less bright. The wife asks, "Why is the light so dim in the house? Did you turn off the lamps?" The husband says, "The light is normal, bright. No one turned anything off."

He does this day after day. As another example, he moves a brooch to another room and then asks, "Where is that brooch I gave you?" She searches, and when she cannot find it, he tells her - look, you moved it here. Moreover, the girl starts to think that she is losing her memory, that she cannot remember anything.

In between turning down the lights, he kisses her, hugs her, and assures her of his love. Meanwhile, the woman starts to doubt herself and thinks that she is crazy and that something is happening to her head. She has no suspicions about her husband, and of course, she is in love with him. The criminal wanted to make her doubt herself by dimming the lights, hoping to gain power over her and then take possession of all her property. Fortunately, clever detectives exposed him, but it was very difficult for the woman to accept the idea that her husband was so cunning - she resisted this thought to the very end.

In the context of a relationship with a narcissist, gaslighting often becomes a disturbingly effective tool used to create a sense of powerlessness and dependency in the victim. This is achieved by denying their experience, withholding information, and dismissing their concerns as overreactions or fabrications.

For example, consider a scenario where one partner consistently denies events that the other clearly remembers, such as a conversation about future commitments or past arguments. The denial is often so assertive and consistent that the victim starts to doubt their memory or sanity. "I never said I would go to that meeting with you; you must have dreamt it!" or "You are overreacting, as usual. I never yelled at you." These statements are typical in the throes of gaslighting, where the reality presented by the narcissist diverges sharply from actual events, causing cognitive dissonance and emotional turmoil in the partner.

The psychological effects of gaslighting are profound and long-lasting. Victims often experience increased anxiety, depression, and an overwhelming sense of confusion. They may feel constantly on edge, doubting not only their memories but their judgments and perceptions as well. Over time, the continuous invalidation of their reality can lead to a diminished sense of self-worth and identity. The manipulative cycle of gaslighting eats away at the individual's ability to make decisions independently, fostering an unhealthy dependency on the narcissist and undermining their mental stability.

In extreme cases, after repeated and prolonged dimming, dissociation phenomena may be observed. They manifest as a feeling that you have stepped out of your body and are observing yourself from the outside. The body becomes somewhat wooden and unresponsive, but there is a sense of peace, even euphoria, in the soul. This is a defense mechanism that helps a victim disconnect from emotional pain and dissociate from feelings. Victims of violence, through the mechanism of dissociation, may develop dissociative identity disorder, where several personalities exist within one person, changing involuntarily, and one personality is unaware of the others. Sometimes, dissociation leads to amnesia.

Recognizing gaslighting when it occurs is pivotal to combating its effects. One effective strategy is to maintain a private record of events and conversations. This can be a digital document or a physical notebook that is kept out of reach of the narcissist. Documenting interactions and experiences provides a factual base that can be referred to when reality seems distorted. It helps reaffirm personal experiences and serves as a grounding tool when confronting the skewed narratives presented by the narcissist.

Moreover, seeking external validation can be crucial. This involves talking to friends, family members, or a therapist who can provide objective perspectives on the situation. These external viewpoints can confirm or question the accuracy of the manipulated reality the narcissist is trying to enforce. Through these external affirmations, victims can begin to see through the fog of gaslighting, regaining trust in their perceptions and judgments.

In terms of countermeasures and protection, setting clear boundaries is critical. This might mean setting limits on the types of behaviors you accept from others or deciding when and how you engage in discussions that have historically led to gaslighting scenarios. Firmly asserting these boundaries during interactions can disrupt the usual pattern of gaslighting. It communicates that the typical manipulations used to distort reality will no longer go unchallenged. Additionally, in situations where gaslighting persists despite setting boundaries, it may become necessary to reconsider the viability of maintaining a relationship where your reality and mental health are continually compromised.

Engaging in self-care practices also plays a vital role in protecting oneself from the effects of gaslighting. Activities that foster a sense of self-worth and personal identity, such as hobbies, social activities, or professional achievements, can reinforce a healthy self-image and reduce susceptibility to manipulation. Regularly participating in activities that remind individuals of their strengths and values can serve as a powerful counterbalance to the effects of being undermined by a narcissistic partner.

In understanding and combating gaslighting, one embarks on the path to reclaiming reality and healing from the psychological scars of manipulation. Recognizing the signs, seeking validation, setting boundaries, and engaging in self-care fortify one's mental fortitude against the subtle yet devastating effects of this manipulative tactic.

"You are no longer fooled, you know. They know that you know. Be prepared to become the enemy."

MARIA CONSIGLIO

Blowing Hot & Cold: Flickering Flames

Blowing hot and cold manipulation is a tactic commonly used by manipulative individuals, including narcissists, to control and confuse their targets. This behavior involves alternating between showing affection, attention, or kindness ("hot") and withdrawing, ignoring, or being distant ("cold"). The purpose of this manipulation is to keep the victim off balance, uncertain, and seeking validation and approval from the manipulator.

When your partner engages in blowing hot and cold manipulation, they go from sweet and loving to distant and critical. They may shower you with love, compliments, and attention, then suddenly become distant, critical, or dismissive. This inconsistency creates a sense of unpredictability and instability in the relationship, causing you to question yourself, your worth, and your perception of reality.

The manipulative partner may start by "love-bombing" you with excessive affection, gifts, and attention to create a strong emotional bond and attachment.

After drawing you in with positive reinforcement, the manipulator may suddenly start criticizing you, leaving you feeling confused and unsure.

The manipulator will use gaslighting tactics to make you doubt your feelings, memories, and perceptions, further destabilizing your sense of reality.

By keeping you on edge and seeking his approval, he maintains a sense of power and control in your relationship.

Blowing hot and cold manipulation is often part of a larger cycle of abuse, where periods of kindness and affection are interspersed with periods of manipulation, control, and emotional abuse.

The cycle of hot and cold behavior creates an emotional rollercoaster for you, leading to feelings of anxiety, insecurity, and emotional turmoil. The constant fluctuations in the manipulator's behavior can be disorienting and emotionally draining.

The manipulator's alternating behavior can cause you to seek validation and approval from him, perpetuating a cycle of dependence and uncertainty. This will slowly erode your self-confidence and autonomy.

Blowing hot and cold manipulation has a detrimental effect on your self-esteem and self-worth. The inconsistent reinforcement of positive and negative behaviors can lead to feelings of inadequacy, self-doubt, and confusion about your value in the relationship.

The manipulator's primary goal in using this tactic is often to maintain control and power in the relationship. By keeping you emotionally invested and unsure of where you stand, the manipulator can manipulate your emotions and actions to serve his interests.

Recognizing this pattern of blowing hot and cold manipulation is key to breaking free from its effects. Understanding that this behavior is a form of emotional manipulation can empower you to set boundaries, seek support, and consider your well-being in the relationship.

Navigating relationships with manipulative individuals who engage in blowing hot and cold behavior can be challenging, but by recognizing the tactics at play and taking proactive steps to protect oneself, individuals can work towards establishing healthier boundaries. Otherwise, such individuals can drain our energy with their ambiguity and leave us shattered. Their selfishness knows no bounds, as they disregard our feelings and value us only when we serve their needs. When they no longer require our presence, they discard us callously, leaving us broken and emotionally depleted. Their lack of remorse or concern for our well-being compounds our pain, making the road to healing long and arduous. Dealing with narcissists often leads to a complete loss of confidence and spirit. The longer we cling to them, the deeper the hurt in the end. Despite our best efforts to salvage the relationship, the inevitable heartbreak awaits. It is crucial to be wary of their charming words and detach ourselves as soon as possible.

I have learned that when a narcissist behaves this way, it is often a form of punishment for perceived disobedience or seeking connections elsewhere. Trying to reason with them or stop their behavior only empowers them further, so it is best to avoid engaging with their manipulative tactics.

Understanding the cyclical nature of narcissistic abuse is crucial, as it is often our hormonal addiction that keeps us entangled in their games. Recognizing these dynamics can help you navigate their behavior more effectively and avoid falling into the trap of frustration.

The push and pull of hot and cold behavior create a predictable cycle of engagement and withdrawal. They lure us in when we distance ourselves and pull away when we seek closeness. This power play indicates their uncertainty about their feelings for us, keeping us on standby while ensuring we remain invested in them. This behavior is an attempt to control the uncontrollable – love - without risking emotional vulnerability. Despite the potential for pain, we often find ourselves drawn to their mixed signals due to cognitive dissonance and the thrill of uncertainty.

Cognitive dissonance, the mental tension of conflicting beliefs, arises when faced with contradictory signals. The struggle to interpret narcissists' actions leaves us feeling anxious and confused, desperate for clarity on their true feelings. The dopamine effect further complicates matters, as the perceived signs of attraction can be exhilarating and addictive. It is essential to question whether our emotions are genuine or simply a result of their manipulative behavior to avoid falling into a deceptive cycle of emotional turmoil.

Individuals who engage in hot and cold behavior are often emotionally unavailable and self-centered, seeking validation and ego boosts rather than genuine connection. It is essential to recognize that their behavior stems from their shortcomings, not from any deficiencies on your part.

Walking away from such dynamics allows you to invest your time and energy in relationships built on honesty, intimacy, and reliability. Games have no place where authenticity and emotional health prevail, making it clear that those who play games are not worthy of your time and energy.

Recovering from the effects of blowing hot and cold manipulation may involve therapy, self-reflection, and self-care practices. Building resilience, trusting one's instincts, and prioritizing mental and emotional well-being are important steps in healing from manipulative relationships.

Neglect: Silent Shadows

Neglect is a commonly used harsh tactic in narcissistic manipulation. In the initial stages of a relationship, particularly in romantic relationships, narcissists appear very involved and attentive. They listen, ask questions, and show genuine interest in you. This behavior is all part of their strategy to draw you in. However, once they feel they have gained control over you, the narcissist may start to ignore you.

This shift can be confusing and hurtful, as illustrated by a client who shared her experience with a narcissistic partner. Initially, the relationship was filled with romance and thoughtful gestures, but as the narcissist gained dominance, the dynamic changed. The once attentive and charming partner became cold and dismissive, leaving their partner feeling unsure and questioning themselves.

One of my friends told me about the development of her relationship with a narcissistic husband: how it started, continued, and ended. In the beginning, everything was very romantic and beautiful: candies, bouquets, gifts, travels. He amazed her with his generosity, thoughtfulness, and attentiveness. Promises flowed like a horn of plenty. The narcissist worked hard to create the perfect image. He immediately wanted to live together. Relationships with a narcissist usually develop very rapidly, which, by the way, is one of the typical signs of a narcissist. After a short time, they moved in together, and then everything changed. The man got what he wanted; she was completely submissive to him, and he no longer needed to create his image and woo her. Instead of attention and conversations, a heavy, oppressive silence set in, and ignoring began. The narcissist frowned, became angry, and did not even greet her in the morning. Coming home from work, he would not ask her how she was, grumbled something, and went to read the newspaper. The woman walked around him, thinking, "What did I do wrong? Maybe I offended him? Maybe I turned the wrong way? Maybe I forgot something?" Nevertheless, if she asked him, "Did I do something wrong? Why are you so dissatisfied?" he would reply, "No, everything is fine. What are you imagining?"

The narcissist's behavior of ignoring and showing dissatisfaction becomes the new norm, creating a tense and unbalanced atmosphere in the relationship. The so called "Silent Treatment" is a particular tactic rather than a comprehensive lack of care. This pattern of manipulation and emotional abuse is a common trait of narcissistic individuals, who thrive on exerting power and control over their partners.

Victims of narcissists often experience feelings of depression and hopelessness, as the narcissist's ignoring behavior leaves them feeling cold and guilty. They struggle to understand the sudden changes in the relationship, trying to decode the narcissist's moods and behavior while feeling like they need to fix themselves. However, these efforts prove futile. It is crucial to realize that the narcissist's coldness is not your fault. They cannot truly love and want to drain your emotional energy to fill their void.

Interrupting someone during a conversation is another form of ignoring them. Why does a narcissist interrupt you? What does this behavior indicate, and how can you address it? Interrupting is a way for the narcissist to assert dominance, signaling that their information holds more weight than yours. It also reflects a lack of empathy and an inability to recognize the emotional effect of their actions on others. Furthermore, it serves as a means of belittling or devaluing your contribution, effectively diminishing your worth. These three behaviors - manipulation, devaluation, and lack of empathy - are all hallmarks of narcissistic tendencies.

Remember, no amount of love you give them will ever be enough. It is important to prioritize your well-being and self-esteem by distancing yourself from the narcissist. If leaving the relationship immediately is not an option, focus on your activities and well-being rather than trying to understand or change the narcissist. Eventually, the narcissist may temporarily revert to a more affectionate state, but this is short-lived, and they will likely return to their cold and distant behavior. It is best to seek ways to end such draining and unproductive relationships as soon as possible.

"Because of indifference, one dies before one actually dies."

ELIE WIESEL

Isolation: Echoes of Solitude

Narcissists often isolate their victims to gain control, foster dependency, and maintain power in the relationship. By isolating their victims from support, resources, and alternative views of family and friends, narcissists can manipulate and exploit them more effectively.

Isolating the victim allows narcissists to exert greater control over the victim's thoughts, emotions, and actions. By taking over the victim's time and cutting off the victim's ties with friends and family members, the narcissist can create a sense of dependency in the victim, making the victim more reliant on the narcissist for validation and security.

Narcissists often seek to maintain a distorted reality in which their perspective is the only valid one. By isolating the victim, the narcissist can prevent the victim from receiving alternative viewpoints that challenge their manipulative tactics or abusive behavior.

Narcissists thrive on emotional manipulation and dependency. This emotional dependency makes it harder for the victim to break free from the narcissist's control. This also makes a victim more susceptible to the narcissist's gaslighting and manipulation. Without external validation and support, the victims may begin to doubt their perceptions, feelings, and worth, further reinforcing the narcissist's control.

Isolation becomes a tool to instill fear and a sense of obligation in the victim. Narcissists can easily make the victim feel trapped, powerless, and dependent on them for their well-being and survival.

In some cases, narcissists may actively work to sabotage the victim's relationships with others by spreading rumors, lies, or misinformation. By tarnishing the victim's reputation or credibility, the narcissist can isolate them from friends, family, and colleagues, further solidifying their control over the victim.

To achieve all this, narcissists may control or monitor the victim's communication channels, such as phone calls, emails, or social media, to limit their interactions with others. Crises of jealousy and triangulation will slowly help them reduce the victim's interaction with the outside world. Narcissists may initiate isolation gradually, making it seem like a natural progression in the relationship. They may subtly discourage the victim from spending time with friends or family, creating distance and weakening external connections over time. Narcissists may use emotional blackmail to keep the victim isolated.

Narcissists are skilled at manipulating the emotions of their victims. By alternating between love bombing and emotional abuse, they create a sense of dependency and confusion in the victim, making it harder for them to recognize and break free from the toxic dynamic relationship.

Financial Control becomes an important tool used to further isolate the victim. Narcissists may exert control over the victim's finances to limit their independence and freedom. By restricting access to money or resources, narcissists can further isolate their victims and make it difficult for them to seek help or escape the abusive relationship.

In some cases, narcissists may use threats, intimidation, or physical violence to keep their victims isolated and under control. The fear of repercussions or harm can prevent victims from seeking help or reaching out to others for support.

Narcissists may alternate between periods of intense affection and cruel behavior, creating the "cycle of abuse." This pattern can keep the victim emotionally invested in the relationship, even as they experience isolation and mistreatment.

Narcissists often create a sense of dependency in their victims by positioning themselves as the sole source of love, validation, and security. By isolating the victim from external sources of support, the narcissist can reinforce this dependency and make it harder for the victim to imagine life without them.

The so-called "learned helplessness" is a psychological phenomenon where an individual comes to believe that they have no control over their circumstances, leading them to passively accept negative treatment from their abuser, preventing them from searching for solutions even when there are opportunities for change or improvement. This concept was first introduced by psychologists Martin Seligman and Steven Maier in the 1960s through a series of experiments involving dogs.

In the initial experiments, dogs were placed in a situation where they received electric shocks that they could not escape. Eventually, the dogs stopped trying to avoid the shocks, even when they were presented with the opportunity to do so. This behavior was attributed to the dogs learning that their actions had no impact on the outcome, leading them to become passive and helpless in the face of adversity.

Learned Helplessness: The Silent Consequence of Isolation

The primary goal of a Narcissist is to foster control by increasing your dependency. Learned helplessness can manifest in various aspects of an individual's life, including relationships, work, and personal challenges. Individuals experiencing learned helplessness often believe that they have no control over their circumstances or outcomes, leading them to adopt a passive approach to challenges. Repeated experiences of failure or adversity can reinforce this belief.

It can result in a lack of motivation or effort to change one's situation, as individuals may feel that their actions will not make a difference. This can further lead to a sense of resignation and apathy towards personal goals or aspirations.

Individuals may engage in avoidance behavior to protect themselves from conflicts or any negative reaction from their abuser.

Learned helplessness has been linked to an increased risk of developing mental health issues such as depression, anxiety, and feelings of hopelessness. The persistent belief that one is powerless to change their circumstances can have a detrimental effect on mental well-being.

Eventually, narcissists isolate their victims to maintain control, foster dependency, and manipulate their emotions and perceptions. By cutting off external connections, narcissists can effectively exploit and abuse their victims without interference. In such situations, the victims need to keep their hobbies and cycle of friends to maintain their connections with family and, more importantly, with reality.

The Blame Game: Projection, Blame-Shifting, and More

Narcissists often employ a complex array of psychological tools to maintain dominance, control, and self-esteem while deflecting any personal accountability. Among these, projection stands out as the primary defense mechanism. Projection involves the narcissist attributing their undesirable feelings, thoughts, or traits to another person, typically the victim. This not only allows them to deny the existence of those qualities in themselves but also to blame others for their internal conflicts. For instance, unfaithful narcissists may accuse their partners of infidelity, creating confusion and making their partners doubt their perceptions and fidelity. This tactic serves multiple purposes: it diverts attention from the actual issues, evokes guilt in the partner, and justifies the narcissist's problematic behavior.

Blame-shifting is closely related to projection but involves a more direct manipulation. Narcissists use this technique to avoid taking responsibility for their actions by continuously redirecting the blame towards others. When confronted with mistakes or misdeeds, narcissists will often immediately find a way to blame their partners or someone close to them. For example, if narcissists fail to meet a work deadline, they might blame their partner for not providing a quiet enough environment at home, even if the partner is not involved. This not only absolves the narcissist of responsibility but also puts the accused on the defensive, shifting the focus away from the original issue.

Before delving further into the narrative, it is worth mentioning that individuals with malicious intent, such as criminals, sexual abusers, and those with NPD, use this manipulative strategy to evade responsibility and accountability for their actions.

The acronym DARVO, which stands for deny, attack, and reverse victim and offender, encapsulates a common tactic that psychological abusers use when confronted with allegations of misconduct. This insidious strategy involves a calculated effort to shift blame onto the victim, distorting the truth and portraying the victim as the wrongdoer instead.

The first step in DARVO is denial, where the perpetrators steadfastly refute any allegations of wrongdoing, often downplaying the effects of their actions and dismissing the victim's feelings. Subsequently, the attackers resort to attacking the victim's character and credibility, launching personal assaults and dredging up past incidents in an attempt to discredit the victim's claims.

Gaslighting, a form of psychological manipulation aimed at sowing doubt and confusion in the victim's mind, is commonly employed during this stage to further undermine the victim's perception of reality and invalidate their experiences.

Moreover, perpetrators may resort to reversing the roles of victim and offender, falsely portraying the victim as the instigator of the abuse. By painting the victim as the antagonist, the abusers seek to deflect blame, avoid consequences, and perpetuate a narrative that exonerates them from any blame.

It is imperative to recognize the insidious nature of DARVO to combat and prevent abusive behavior and empower ourselves and others to identify and address instances of psychological abuse.

In addition to projection and blame-shifting, narcissists often use more intricate tactics, like triangulation, scapegoating, and the creation of flying monkeys. Triangulation involves the use of a third party to validate the narcissist's viewpoints and to undermine the victim. By bringing another person into the dynamics of the relationship, the narcissist creates confusion and fosters an atmosphere of competition and insecurity. For instance, narcissists might tell a friend in the presence of their partner how supportive and understanding the friend is, implicitly criticizing the partner's lack of support, thereby creating tension and doubt in the partner.

Scapegoating is another tool that narcissists use to pin all the negative outcomes and faults onto a particular individual, often someone within their family or workplace. This process not only allows the narcissist to feel superior by comparison but also rallies others to their side against the scapegoat. In a family setting, this might manifest as a narcissistic parent constantly blaming one child for household tensions, diverting attention from the real issues within the family dynamics.

Lastly, the creation of flying monkeys involves the narcissist manipulating others to do their bidding, often without the third party realizing it. These individuals are used to spread gossip, carry messages, or do harm on behalf of the narcissist, all while the narcissist maintains plausible deniability. For instance, a narcissist might subtly hint to a mutual friend about their partner's supposed faults without directly engaging themselves, thus spreading doubt and mistrust within their social circle, reinforcing the narcissist's fabricated narratives, and isolating the victim.

Recognizing these tactics is the first step in countering them. Awareness allows the victim to see these behaviors as they are happening and to distinguish them from normal relational conflicts. This understanding can significantly reduce the confusion and self-doubt that these tactics are designed to evoke. To effectively counter these behaviors, setting firm boundaries is crucial. This involves clearly communicating what is acceptable and what is not and consistently enforcing these boundaries, which helps to protect against manipulation.

Additionally, seeking external perspectives can be invaluable. Consulting with friends, family, or a professional who is not under the narcissist's influence can provide a reality check and help validate the victim's experiences and perceptions. This external validation is often key in maintaining one's understanding of the truth in the face of persistent narcissistic manipulation.

In dealing with a narcissist, knowledge of these tactics and an understanding of how to counter them can empower victims to regain control of their interactions and their emotional well-being, reducing the effects of the narcissist's manipulative behaviors.

"Have you ever gotten in a fight with someone because you told them what was bothering you, and instead of them apologizing, they find a way to make you feel bad about it. So you are left regretting even saying anything."

MARIA CONSIGLIO

1.4 COVERT VS. OVERT NARCISSISTS: UNDERSTANDING THE DIFFERENT FACADES

Narcissism, as a spectrum of behaviors, manifests in two primary forms that are crucial to distinguish: the covert and the overt narcissist. Each type influences relationships differently and requires the victims to utilize a tailored approach. Understanding the nuanced behaviors of both can significantly enhance your ability to manage a relationship with a narcissist, whether in personal interactions or broader social contexts.

Covert narcissists, often referred to as vulnerable narcissists, present a facade that contradicts the classic narcissistic persona. They may not exude confidence; instead, they often appear shy, sensitive, or withdrawn. This demeanor, however, masks a deep-seated sense of entitlement and self-centeredness. Covert narcissists harbor feelings of inadequacy and often rely on the sympathy and validation of others to bolster their self-esteem. Unlike their overt counterparts, they do not overtly demand admiration or attention, but they feel equally entitled to it and may become quietly resentful if they feel they are not receiving their 'due.' For instance, if overlooked for a promotion, a covert narcissist might not openly confront the issue but could harbor a long-term grudge, subtly undermining colleagues or downplaying the achievements of others.

Their tactics of manipulation are often passive. Covert narcissists are likely to play the victim or use guilt to bind others to them. They manipulate not through overt dominance but through fostering a sense of obligation or pity in their partners or peers. This can make their manipulation harder to recognize and, therefore, more insidious, as they often cultivate an image of being misunderstood or undervalued. Dealing with a covert narcissist requires a careful balance of empathy and boundary-setting. It is crucial to validate their feelings when appropriate without enabling their sense of entitlement or dependency. For those entangled in a relationship with a covert narcissist, consistent and firm boundaries are essential, as is a focus on not getting drawn into their narrative of victimhood.

In contrast, covert narcissists align with the traditional image of narcissistic personality disorder. They are characterized by grandiosity, a demand for constant admiration, and a distinct lack of empathy. Overt narcissists are often domineering, aggressively pursuing their desires and ambitions and openly manipulating others to achieve their ends. They thrive on attention and are often charismatic and seductive, drawing people into their orbit with charm and confidence. However, this charm can quickly reveal a darker side as they use their influence to exploit others without remorse. An overt narcissist, for example, might publicly belittle a partner to maintain control or to demonstrate their power to others, using humiliation as a tool to tether their partner closely to them.

Dealing with covert narcissists requires a robust strategy of self-protection and assertiveness. Unlike the covert narcissist, whose manipulations might be more emotional and less visible, the overt narcissist's actions are usually clear and present. It is vital to avoid getting caught in the web of their charisma by maintaining a strong sense of self and firm personal boundaries. Strategies might include limiting personal information shared with the narcissist to avoid giving them ammunition for future manipulation and maintaining a strong support network to help validate your experiences and perceptions.

The two different types can have profoundly different effects on relationships. Covert narcissists might cause their partners to feel a constant sense of guilt and obligation, leading to a draining and emotionally enervating relationship. In contrast, relationships with overt narcissists often involve cycles of intense admiration and equally intense devaluation, creating an emotional roller-coaster that can be both addictive and devastating.

Recognizing whether a narcissist is covert or overt can profoundly affect how you handle these relationships. Each requires a different approach, with a focus on understanding the underlying motivations and behaviors that drive them. For those dealing with covert narcissists, recognizing the subtle signs of manipulation and maintaining emotional distance is key. For those dealing with overt narcissists, building and enforcing boundaries to protect against their more blatant exploitations is crucial. In both cases, safeguarding one's self-esteem and emotional health is paramount, requiring constant vigilance and a strong sense of self to navigate these challenging interpersonal dynamics effectively.

1.5 NARCISSISTIC SUPPLY: WHAT IT IS AND WHY IT MATTERS

Understanding the concept of narcissistic supply is fundamental to grasping how narcissists operate within relationships. Essentially, narcissistic supply refers to the sustenance that feeds narcissists' egos, maintaining their self-esteem and regulating their self-worth. Unlike healthy emotional exchanges in relationships, narcissistic supply is characterized by its exploitative and depleting nature, serving primarily to affirm the narcissist's grandiose self-image. This supply can be derived from various sources, each serving to inflate the narcissist's sense of superiority and control.

Common sources of narcissistic supply include but are not limited to excessive admiration from romantic partners, accolades and achievements in professional environments, and social acknowledgment and prestige. Each of these sources reinforces the narcissist's crafted public and private personas, underpinning their often-fragile self-esteem. For instance, in romantic relationships, narcissists may demand constant attention and validation, using the partners' devotion to bolster their ego. In the workplace, they might seek to achieve not only career advancement but also the recognition that accompanies such successes, which feeds into their self-perceived exceptionalism.

The role of the partner in providing narcissistic supply is both pivotal and, unfortunately, detrimental. Partners of narcissists often find themselves in the unenviable position of constant giver, continuously feeding the narcissist's need for admiration and attention without reciprocation. This dynamic is not always apparent initially; it unfolds as the narcissist gradually conditions their partner to prioritize the narcissist's emotional needs over their own. Partners may be showered with affection and attention when the supply is plentiful but may face coldness or punishment when they fail to meet the narcissist's demands. This conditioning can tether the partner closely to the narcissist, often at the cost of the partner's emotional health and self-esteem.

It can be easy to fall into patterns of enabling a narcissistic behavior, whether you are trying to protect yourself from further attack. Sometimes it may seem easier to lay low and avoid a fight. However, such behavior will only strengthen the power of the Narcissist over you.

Strategically minimizing one's role as a supplier to a narcissist involves recognizing and understanding these dynamics. Awareness is the first step. Identifying the ways you might be contributing to this supply can help gradually reduce the amount of emotional energy you invest in satisfying the narcissist's needs. This might include setting firmer boundaries around your time and emotional resources or consciously redirecting your focus toward your own needs and interests. It is important to note, however, that reducing narcissistic supply can sometimes lead to increased attempts by the narcissist to regain control. Therefore, these strategies should be employed with caution and, ideally, with support from a therapist or support group familiar with narcissistic behaviors.

Moreover, fostering a sense of self that is independent of the narcissist's validation is crucial. Engaging in activities and relationships that reinforce your worth and reduce your emotional dependency on the narcissist can gradually diminish their influence. Cultivating a strong support network and pursuing personal interests can help restore a sense of individuality and purpose that the relationship with the narcissist may have eroded. This process is not about confrontation but about quietly reinforcing your boundaries and sense of self, which can naturally decrease the supply you provide.

Additionally, communication about your boundaries can be crucial. Clearly articulating your limits and sticking to them can help manage the narcissist's expectations and your role in their emotional ecosystem. This might mean stating plainly that you need time for yourself or that certain demands are unreasonable. While this may initially provoke resistance, consistency in your boundaries can lead to a gradual shift in dynamics. It is essential, however, to approach this with realistic expectations and an understanding of the potential challenges that may arise as the narcissist adjusts to the new norms.

In the broader sense, minimizing your role as a supplier does not mean neglecting the emotional needs of your partner but rather fostering a healthier, more balanced relationship dynamic. This balance can only be achieved, however, when both partners are willing to engage in honest self-reflection and mutual respect. For those involved with a narcissist, this often requires external support, and it may sometimes lead to the realization that a healthy dynamic is not achievable. In such cases, the decision to step back or leave the relationship entirely may become necessary for personal well-being.

Navigating a relationship with a narcissist is undoubtedly challenging, particularly in terms of managing the complex dynamics of narcissistic supply. However, with the right strategies and support, it is possible to reclaim your emotional autonomy and reduce the effects of narcissistic behaviors on your life. Whether through setting boundaries, cultivating independence, or seeking external support, the goal is to foster a sense of self that is robust enough to withstand the pressures of the narcissistic relationship, ultimately leading to healthier interactions and personal growth.

1.6 WHY NARCISSISTS RETURN: CYCLES AND ESCALATION

Narcissists may return to their victims. Most of them keep their victims on a hook and continue to manipulate, exploit, and control them even after their relationship is over. Narcissists keep all their victims within reach for various reasons, often driven by their need for control, validation, and narcissistic supply. The cycle of idealization, devaluation, and discard commonly seen in narcissistic relationships can lead to a pattern of intermittent reinforcement that keeps the victim emotionally invested and vulnerable to the narcissist's manipulative tactics. Here are some reasons why narcissists may return to their victims:

Narcissists are constantly in need of a narcissistic supply. When they feel a lack of this supply or experience a perceived threat to their ego, they may return to a previous victim to regain a sense of power and control. They may return to their victims to boost their ego and sense of self-worth. Rekindling a past relationship may validate their desirability, attractiveness, or power over others.

Narcissists are skilled at manipulating the emotions of their victims to serve their own needs. By alternating between periods of idealization and devaluation, they create a sense of emotional turmoil and confusion in their victims, making it easier to lure them back into the relationship.

Returning to a previous victim allows narcissists to assert control and power over individuals. By rekindling the relationship, narcis-sists can maintain dominance and manipulate their victims' emotions and behaviors to suit their agenda. Hoovering is a manipulation tactic narcissists use to draw their victims back into the relationship after a period of discard or estrangement. By showering victims with affection, promises of change, or apologies, narcissists aim to reestablish their hold over their victims and maintain their source of narcissistic supply.

Some narcissists may fear being alone or abandoned, leading them to cycle back to familiar relationships for a sense of security and stability, especially if something goes wrong in their new relationship. Returning to a previous victim may provide a temporary sense of comfort and control for the narcissist.

Do not forget that narcissists often lack empathy and the ability to consider the feelings and well-being of others. Their return to a victim may be driven solely by their own needs and desires, without regard for the victim's emotional state or well-being. Narcissists often view their victims as possessions or extensions of themselves. Returning to a previous victim may be driven by a desire to reclaim ownership and control over the individual, treating them as an object to be manipulated and used for their benefit.

Narcissists are adept at using manipulation tactics to exploit and control others. Returning to their victims allows narcissists to continue playing mind games, gaslighting, and emotionally manipulating the individual to maintain their power and dominance in the relationship.

Remember that the cycle of abuse in narcissistic relationships typically involves periods of idealization, devaluation, and discard. The narcissists' return to their victims may be part of this repetitive cycle, with the victims being drawn back into the relationship by promises of change or false hope for a better future and keeping them emotionally entangled and vulnerable to further mistreatment.

I know couples who keep on separating and getting back together over and over through decades...

Every new cycle leads to an escalation. Escalation is dangerous because your partner is showing you that he or she can use new and more damaging tactics to continue to hoard power and control in the relationship. Abusers may test whether they can get away with crossing a line that has never been crossed before to create a new and deeper level of power and control when they fear they are losing it.

Many survivors who reach out to The Hotline express shock and disbelief at the severity of the abuse they have endured in their relationships. It often takes a terrifying event for them to realize the danger they are in, prompting them to seek help and take action to protect themselves, their children, or their pets. The fear they experience is a powerful motivator to break free from the cycle of abuse and prevent further harm.

It is crucial to validate this fear and recognize that survivors are often the best judges when a situation has become truly dangerous. This spontaneous moment of realization can be a turning point that alters the course of their lives. If you sense that the abuse in your relationship is escalating, understanding the signs of escalation is the key to protecting yourself and your loved ones from further harm. Trust your instincts and prioritize your safety above all else.

Victims of narcissistic abuse need to recognize the manipulative tactics of the narcissist and not get fooled that a narcissist may change. NPD is a complex and challenging mental health condition that cannot be "cured" in the traditional sense. However, therapy and other interventions can help individuals with the disorder manage symptoms and improve relationships.

Individuals with NPD may resist seeking treatment due to their inflated sense of self-importance and lack of insights into their behavior. Cognitive-behavioral therapy (CBT), psychodynamic therapy, and schema therapy are common approaches used to help individuals with NPD explore their thoughts, emotions, and behaviors, develop self-awareness, and learn healthier ways of relating to others.

Treating NPD can be challenging due to narcissists' resistance to acknowledge their shortcomings and the effects of their behavior on others. It may require a long-term commitment to therapy and a willingness to explore deep-seated issues related to self-esteem, relationships, and emotional regulation.

Therapy for NPD often focuses on addressing underlying issues, such as low self-esteem, insecurity, and the need for external validation. By exploring these core issues and developing healthier coping mechanisms, individuals with NPD can work towards building more authentic and fulfilling relationships.

One of the key goals of therapy for NPD is to help individuals develop empathy and a greater understanding of the perspectives and feelings of others. By learning to recognize and validate the emotions of others, individuals with NPD can improve their interpersonal skills and cultivate more meaningful connections.

While there is no specific medication to treat NPD, psychiatric medications, such as antidepressants or mood stabilizers, may be prescribed to address co-occurring mental health conditions, such as depression or anxiety, that often accompany NPD.

For victims, setting boundaries and focusing on self-care and healing are crucial steps in breaking free from the cycle of abuse and manipulation perpetuated by narcissists.

1.7 CO-DEPENDENCY IN A RELATIONSHIP WITH A NARCISSIST: WHY IS IT SO HARD TO LEAVE

Codependency in relationships with an abuser can be complex and challenging. Codependent individuals may prioritize the needs and desires of their abusers over their well-being, often at the expense of their mental, emotional, and sometimes physical health, while becoming a needed component for the abuser, a source of narcissistic supply.

It may be hard for someone in a codependent relationship with an abuser to leave.

Codependent individuals have already developed a strong emotional attachment to their abusers, making it difficult to imagine their lives without them.

Besides, these individuals often have low self-esteem and may believe they do not deserve better treatment, leading them to stay in harmful relationships.

The idea of being alone or facing the unknown can be terrifying for someone in a codependent relationship, even if the relationship is toxic.

Abusers often use manipulation and control tactics to keep their victims trapped in the relationship, making it hard for the codependent individuals to break free.

In some cases, the codependent individuals may be financially dependent on their abusers, making it challenging to leave without a plan or support system in place.

Abusers may isolate their victims from friends, family, and other sources of support, leaving the codependent individuals feeling like they have nowhere to turn.

Codependent individuals may hold on to the hope that the abuser will change their behavior despite evidence to the contrary.

It is important to understand that in abusive relationships, a phenomenon known as trauma bonding occurs, where the victim forms a strong emotional bond with the abuser as a result of the cycle of abuse and intermittent reinforcement of positive behaviors.

Codependent individuals may experience feelings of guilt and shame about the abusive relationship, which can make it difficult for them to seek help or leave the situation.

Over time, the abusive behavior may become normalized in the codependent individual's mind, making it even harder for them to recognize the severity of the situation and take action to leave.

Abusers may threaten or intimidate their victims to prevent them from leaving, instilling fear of retaliation or harm if the victim attempts to break free from the relationship.

Codependent individuals may lack a strong support system or feel isolated, which can make it harder for them to seek help or resources to leave the abusive relationship.

The codependent individuals may be so enmeshed in the relationship dynamics that they struggle to envision a life outside of it, leading to a sense of dependency on the abuser, just like a bird that has lived in a cage for a long time and does not fly out of the cage once you open it.

Individuals in codependent relationships with abusers need to prioritize their safety and well-being, concentrate on creating a path toward leaving the abusive relationship, and establish healthier boundaries. Remember that you deserve to be treated with respect and care, and there are resources available to assist you in making positive changes in your life.

CHAPTER 2
INSIDE THE NARCISSISTIC RELATIONSHIP

The allure of a new relationship can be intoxicating, especially when it starts with an overwhelming outpouring of affection and attention. This whirlwind experience, often characterized by grand romantic gestures and declarations of love, can sweep you off your feet. However, when these over-the-top expressions continue to escalate rapidly and early in the relationship, it might not be the fairytale it seems. This phenomenon, known as "love bombing," is a common tactic used by narcissists to captivate and control their partners. Understanding this manipulative strategy is crucial for those who find themselves dazzled by someone's seemingly undying affection, as it may be the first thread in a complex web of emotional manipulation.

2.1 LOVE BOMBING: INITIAL CHARMS AND EARLY WARNING SIGNS

Love bombing might feel like genuine affection and the kind of storybook romance everyone dreams of, but it has a much darker side. It occurs when someone overwhelms you with loving words, actions, and behaviors as a manipulation technique. The intensity is the key here. Specifically, love bombing is not just about being romantic or thoughtful; it is an onslaught of affection and atten-tion that is designed to "bomb" you into compliance and lower your psychological defenses.

The purpose of love bombing is to create an emotional depen-dency that makes you more susceptible to future manipulation. It is like the setup in a long con: the narcissist builds up this perfect persona and the ultimate loving relationship, making it harder for you to leave later when their true colors start to show. Imagine receiving flowers every day, constant texts and calls, all your favorite foods, and heart-stopping compliments that seem to see right into your soul - all strategically deployed to win over your complete trust and affection.

Distinguishing Genuine Affection from Manipulation

To differentiate between love bombing and genuine affection, you need to look at the consistency, intensity, and timing of the behavior. Love bombing often feels overwhelming, and it can appear very early in a relationship, creating a sense of unease that things are moving too quickly. In contrast, genuine affection builds gradually and is based on mutual respect and interest rather than an over-powering one-sided onslaught.

For example, if someone listens to you talk about how much you love a certain book and later gifts you the first edition, that is thoughtful and shows they care about your interests. However, if someone starts texting you multiple times a day, quickly professes deep feelings, and pushes you to move the relationship forward at an uncomfortable speed after just one date, these are red flags. The key difference lies in respect for boundaries: genuine affec-tion respects your pace, while love bombing tries to sweep you off your feet by force.

Early Warning Signs

Subtle signs can alert you to the fact that you are being love-bombed. A significant warning is the feeling that the relationship is on a fast track without your consent. You might feel like things are just "too good to be true" or that the emotional intimacy being expressed does not match the short time you have been together. Another sign is if disagreements or boundaries are ignored or met with over-the-top acts of affection to smooth over any dissent.

For instance, you might express a desire to spend some time focusing on personal projects or with friends, but the narcissist will insist on spending more and more time together, perhaps showing up uninvited or with extravagant gifts to persuade you to cancel your plans. This disrespect for personal boundaries is a hallmark of love bombing meant to tether you closely to them.

Protective Measures

To protect yourself from being overwhelmed by love bombing, it is essential to set and enforce clear boundaries early in the relationship. Communicate openly about your needs and pace for a relationship, and watch carefully how the other person respects these. Slowing down the pace can help as well, giving you more time to carefully assess the other person's motives and build a relationship based on shared respect rather than emotional dependency.

Moreover, maintain your social connections and hobbies. Narcissists often aim to isolate their targets to gain more control. By keeping up with your regular activities and seeing friends and family, you retain your support network and perspective, which can provide a vital reality check against the distorted affection from a narcissist.

Educating yourself about narcissistic behaviors and trusting your instincts are also crucial. If something feels off, it often is. Consulting with trusted friends or a therapist can provide clarity and support, helping you navigate your feelings and the relationship dynamics more effectively. Remember, real love should feel secure and comfortable, not overwhelming and coercive. By recognizing the signs of love bombing and taking steps to protect your emotional well-being, you can guard against manipulation and foster healthier, more genuine relationships.

2.2 THE CYCLE OF ABUSE: RECOGNIZING PATTERNS IN A NARCISSISTIC RELATIONSHIP

Understanding the cyclical pattern of abuse in a relationship with a narcissist can be both enlightening and distressing. Generally, this cycle can be broken down into three distinct phases: idealization, devaluation, and discard. Each phase plays a critical role in the manipulative dynamics that characterize narcissistic abuse, and recognizing these can be the first step toward breaking free from their destructive loop.

Phases of the Narcissistic Abuse Cycle

The **idealization phase** often sets the stage for the cycle. During this period, narcissists shower their partners with attention, affection, and admiration. This phase is marked by intense romance and charm, with the narcissists presenting their best selves. They seem to be the perfect partner, often mirroring your deepest desires and interests. However, this is a calculated move to secure your attachment and devotion. It is not about a genuine connection but about anchoring their ability to manipulate you later.

Transitioning from idealization, the **devaluation phase** emerges when the narcissists begin to feel secure in their control over the relationship. Gradually or suddenly, the warmth and affection they previously expressed turn into criticism and contempt. You might find yourself constantly demeaned, gaslighted, and made to feel inadequate. During this phase, the narcissists' true self starts to surface more consistently, revealing a stark contrast to the person they initially appeared to be. The shift can be jarring, as the praise they once freely gave turns into relentless nitpicking, undermining your self-esteem and destabilizing your sense of reality.

The final phase, **discard**, occurs when the narcissists feel they have sufficiently exploited their partners' usefulness or when maintaining the relationship becomes too cumbersome for them. In this phase, the narcissist may abruptly end the relationship or gradually withdraw their attention and affection, leaving you feeling discarded and worthless. This phase is often cyclical, with the narcissist potentially reinitiating contact later, leading to a renewed cycle of abuse.

Examples of Each Phase

Consider a scenario where, during the idealization phase, a partner regularly plans elaborate date nights, praises your every attribute, and aligns with all your interests, making you feel uniquely understood and valued. As the relationship progresses into devaluation, the same partner may start to criticize how you dress for the dates, dismiss your opinions, and ridicule your interests. Finally, in the discard phase, they might end the relationship suddenly, citing your supposed inadequacies as the reason, only to perhaps return weeks later promising change and reigniting the idealization phase to draw you back in.

Recognizing the Cycle in One's Relationship

To determine whether you are in such a cycle, reflect on the nature of your relationship's progression. Ask yourself: Have there been distinct periods where idealization by your partner was followed by severe criticism or neglect? Do these phases repeat themselves? Keeping a journal can help you track these patterns, offering a clearer view of the cyclic shifts in behavior that characterize your relationship. Additionally, sharing your experiences with trusted friends or a therapist can provide external validation and help you recognize patterns, as you might be too emotionally invested in the relationship to see them clearly.

Breaking the Cycle

Breaking free from the cycle of narcissistic abuse requires a strong resolve and often external support. Begin by setting firm boundaries. Decide what behaviors you will no longer tolerate and stick to your limits. Communicating these boundaries to the narcissist might not change their behavior, but it can empower you to respond differently, for instance, by disengaging or leaving the situation when your boundaries are crossed.

Seeking professional help is also crucial. Therapists who specialize in narcissistic abuse can offer guidance tailored to your situation, helping you understand that the abuse is not your fault and providing strategies to regain your self-esteem and independence. Additionally, support groups, both online and offline, can offer solace and advice from others who have faced similar challenges.

Finally, focus on rebuilding your life. Invest in activities and relationships that reinforce your worth and bring you joy. This process helps in healing from the trauma of the abuse and rebuilding a life that is no longer centered around the narcissistic relationship. Remember, stepping away from such a relationship is not just about ending a partnership but also about beginning a new chapter of self-discovery and recovery.

2.3 HOOVERING AND TRIANGULATION: KEEPING YOU HOOKED

In the realm of relationships tainted by narcissism, 'hoovering' is a metaphor drawn from the familiar household vacuum, signifying how a narcissist attempts to suck a previous partner back into the chaotic whirlwind of the relationship after a period of separation. This tactic typically surfaces when you show signs of moving on or when the narcissist needs your emotional or practical support again. It is characterized by sudden bursts of affection, promises of change, heartfelt apologies, or, sometimes, dire declarations of crisis wherein narcissists portray themselves as the victim needing rescue. These actions are often calculated to trigger your empathy and prompt a sense of obligation or guilt, pulling you back into the dynamics of the relationship even when part of you knows better.

For instance, imagine a scenario where, weeks or months after a breakup, your ex-partner sends you messages expressing how much they have changed, how miserable they feel without you, and how they believe you are truly meant to be together. They might recall specific happy memories or even show up at events you are attending, claiming serendipitous intentions. The underlying goal is not reconciliation borne out of true love or remorse but rather the need to regain control and continue the cycle of abuse.

Hovering is an effective technique for a narcissist to exploit control, create confusion and reinforce dependency.

Triangulation

Triangulation is another insidious technique in the narcissist's manipulation toolkit. It involves the use of a third party to validate the narcissist's perspectives and to create a sense of competition, jealousy, or insecurity in you. By bringing another person into the relationship dynamic, directly or indirectly, the narcissist creates drama and conflict that they then manipulate to their advantage, often reinforcing their desirability and control.

This tactic can manifest in various forms.

Comparison with an Ex: A narcissist may frequently compare their current partner to an ex-partner, highlighting perceived flaws or shortcomings in the present relationship or even calling you by her/his name. By praising the ex-partner's qualities or achievements and telling you stories from their past, the narcissist creates feelings of insecurity and inadequacy in their current partner.

Emotional Affairs: A narcissist may engage in emotional affairs with other individuals, seeking emotional support, validation, or attention outside of the relationship. This emotional connection with a third party can create feelings of jealousy and betrayal in the victim, further fueling the narcissist's control over their emotions.

Triangulation with Family Members or Friends: A narcissist may involve family members or friends in the relationship dynamic, using them as allies to reinforce their point of view or manipulate the victim. By triangulating the opinions and perspectives of others, the narcissist undermines the victim's sense of autonomy and agency.

Flirting with Others: A narcissist may flirt with or show interest in other people in front of their partner, creating feelings of jealousy and insecurity. This behavior is designed to make the victim feel inadequate and to assert the narcissist's control over their emotions.

Gaslighting and Manipulation: In cases of triangulation, a narcissist may gaslight the victim by denying or downplaying the involvement of a third party in the relationship. They may manipulate their victims' perception of reality, making them question their own experiences and feelings.

Creating Rivalries: A narcissist may intentionally create rivalries or competition between their partners or peers, pitting them against each other for attention and validation. By fostering a sense of competition, the narcissist maintains power and control over the individuals involved.

Using Children as Pawns: In co-parenting situations, a narcissist may use children as pawns in triangulation, manipulating custody arrangements or parental responsibilities to gain leverage over the victim. This form of triangulation can have damaging effects on the well-being of both the victim and the children involved.

A narcissist might also confide in a mutual friend about issues between you two, subtly seeking to turn others against you. Each of these actions is designed to undermine your confidence, exploit your emotional vulnerability and to increase your reliance on the narcissist's approval and validation.

Effects of These Tactics

Hoovering and triangulation have profound emotional and psychological effects. These tactics can leave you feeling confused, insecure, and on edge. They erode your sense of self-worth and can significantly impair your ability to trust your judgment. Over time, this can lead to anxiety and depression, as you feel increasingly trapped and powerless in an unpredictable emotional landscape where the narcissist seems to hold all the cards. The stress of navigating these manipulations can also spill over into other areas of your life, affecting your social relationships, work performance, and overall mental health.

Coping Strategies

Dealing with hoovering and triangulation requires a firm resolve and strategic planning. One of the most effective defenses is the no-contact rule. Cutting off all communication with the narcissist prevents them from being able to manipulate your emotions directly. This means blocking their number, email, and social media contacts and possibly making new accounts where they cannot reach you. It is crucial to inform close friends and family about your decision so they can support you in maintaining this boundary.

Maintaining no contact can be challenging, especially if the narcissist uses hoovering tactics that pull at your heartstrings or provoke sympathy. During these times, it is essential to remind yourself why you chose to break free from the relationship. Keeping a journal where you have documented instances of abuse and manipulation can help reinforce your memories of why staying away is beneficial. Additionally, seeking support from therapists who understand narcissistic abuse or joining support groups can provide you with additional coping strategies and validation of your experiences and feelings.

In cases where no contact is entirely possible, such as when co-parenting with a narcissist, setting firm boundaries and limiting communication to necessary topics can help manage interactions. Using communication tools designed for divorced or separated parents, like Talking Parents or My Family Wizard, can keep interactions strictly about parenting, avoiding personal confrontations and reducing the narcissist's opportunities to manipulate your emotions.

Ultimately, the key to successfully navigating and overcoming the tactics of hoovering and triangulation lies in recognizing them for what they are: tools of manipulation used by the narcissist to maintain control over you. By understanding these tactics and preparing yourself emotionally and practically to resist them, you empower yourself to move forward toward healthier relationships and reclaim your autonomy and well-being.

2.4 DISCARD PHASE DYNAMICS: PREPARING FOR THE INEVITABLE LETDOWN

The discard phase is a pivotal and often painful part of the cycle in a relationship with a narcissist. This phase occurs when the narcissists decide that their partners no longer serve their needs or fulfill their desires. It is characterized by a withdrawal of affection and a significant reduction in communication. The shift can be abrupt and disorienting, leaving their discarded partners feeling bewildered and devalued. Understanding this phase is crucial as it often marks the end of the cycle but also the beginning of a potential renewal and healing process for the victim.

One of the most challenging aspects of this phase is the emotional turmoil that accompanies the realization that the relationship was built on a fragile foundation of manipulation and self-interest rather than mutual respect and affection. The narcissists may end the relationship suddenly and without explanation, or they might initiate a series of events that force their partners to leave. This could involve escalating the abuse, infidelity, or emotional withdrawal. The narcissists' goal is to preserve their ego and avoid any responsibility for the relationship's demise, often leaving the discarded partner with unresolved questions and profound self-doubt.

When narcissists are entertaining a new supply, they tend to treat you increasingly poorly. They are preparing themselves for a discard. They need to prove to themselves that leaving you is the right decision, so they devalue you in in the most hurtful ways. In some cases, they may even wish for you to end things first, as it would make their exit less complicated.

Emotional Preparedness

Preparing yourself emotionally for the discard phase involves recognizing the signs that it is approaching. These signs might include a noticeable decrease in the narcissist's communication, an increase in criticism, or an outright expression of disinterest in things that concern you. You might also notice the narcissist forming new relationships or rekindling old ones as they prepare to transition their attention and manipulation to a new source of narcissistic supply.

To brace yourself for this phase, it is essential to start distancing your emotions from the relationship. Begin by reaffirming your self-worth and focusing on your happiness independent of the narcissist. Engaging in activities that boost your self-esteem and reconnecting with friends and family can reinforce your support network and remind you of your value outside of the relationship. Additionally, seeking therapy can provide a safe space to express your feelings and receive professional guidance on navigating the emotional complexities of the discard phase.

Handling the Aftermath

A whirlwind of emotions often marks the immediate aftermath of being discarded. Confusion, grief, anger, and relief might all surface as you process the end of the relationship. Managing these emotions is key to your recovery and can be achieved through various means of self-care and external support.

First, allow yourself to grieve the loss of the relationship. It is natural to feel sadness and loss, even if the relationship was harmful. Acknowledging your feelings without judgment can facilitate healing. During this time, maintaining no contact with the narcissist is crucial. Continued interaction can lead to emotional setbacks and prolong the pain.

Practically, you may need to untangle your life from that of the narcissist. This might involve financial separation, dividing shared assets, or navigating co-parenting if children are involved. Each step should be handled legally and formally, with clear boundaries to prevent any manipulation or abuse.

Furthermore, investing in your physical health is also vital. Regular exercise, a nutritious diet, and sufficient sleep can improve your mood and energy levels, making it easier to handle the stress and emotional strain of the situation.

Learning From the Experience

While painful, the discard phase offers invaluable lessons about personal strength, resilience, and the dynamics of healthy relationships. Reflecting on the relationship can help you identify red flags that you may have missed or ignored and understand the patterns that led you into the narcissistic relationship. This reflection can be crucial in making healthier relationship choices in the future.

One effective way to utilize the experience for personal growth is through journaling. Writing about your experiences can clarify your thoughts and feelings, helping you analyze the relationship more objectively. Identify the qualities that drew you to the narcissist and consider how these can be better directed towards healthier relationships.

Recognizing the importance of boundaries is crucial. Your experience with a narcissist likely taught you the consequences of boundary violations. Moving forward, you can apply this understanding by setting firmer boundaries in all your relationships, ensuring that your needs and well-being are adequately respected and prioritized.

Lastly, consider sharing your experiences with others, either through support groups or informal discussions. Sharing not only helps others who might be in similar situations but can also reinforce your understanding and resolution. Engaging with a community of people who have gone through similar experiences can be incredibly affirming and healing.

In conclusion, while the discard phase is an undeniably painful part of ending a relationship with a narcissist, it also marks the beginning of a journey toward healing and self-discovery. By understanding and preparing for this phase, handling its aftermath effectively, and learning from the experience, you can emerge stronger, wiser, and more equipped for healthier relationships in the future.

2.5 EMOTIONAL ROLLER COASTER: OXYTOCIN, DOPAMINE, CORTISOL

In abusive relationships, a form of hormonal codependency can often be at play. This phenomenon involves the interplay of hormones, such as oxytocin, dopamine, and cortisol, which can contribute to the cycle of abuse and the difficulty of breaking free from toxic dynamics.

The key player in this emotional roller coaster is a hormone known as dopamine. This neurotransmitter plays a crucial role in keeping us hooked on our abuser, as it drives us to seek rewards and feel pleasure in response to perceived gratification. Dating, in essence, is a game of rewards, with attention and emotional connection serving as the sought-after prizes. When dopamine floods our system, we experience a rush of endorphins, leading us to seek out the actions that trigger these pleasurable feelings.

The science of dopamine secretion reveals that the mere anticipation of a reward can trigger its release. Moreover, uncertainty amplifies this effect, doubling the dopamine high. In situations where mixed signals leave us unsure of the other person's feelings, this neurochemical surge becomes addictive, fueling our desire to keep investing in the relationship despite the ambiguity. We are drawn to behaviors that make us feel good, even if they also bring about negative emotions—a phenomenon known as cognitive dissonance. We convince ourselves that the potential reward justifies enduring uncertainty and emotional turmoil.

Oxytocin, dopamine, and cortisol are three key hormones that play significant roles in regulating emotions, social bonding, stress responses, and reward processing in relationships.

Oxytocin

Oxytocin, often referred to as the "love hormone," is released during positive social interactions, intimacy, and bonding. In abusive relationships, the abuser may alternate between moments of affection and cruelty, leading to a surge of oxytocin during the loving moments. This hormone can create a sense of attachment and loyalty to the abuser, making it challenging for the victim to leave the relationship despite the harmful behavior. Oxytocin is released during activities such as hugging, kissing, cuddling, and sexual intimacy to strengthen emotional bonds and foster feelings of closeness and security.

Although oxytocin has been linked to positive relationship behaviors, such as empathy, communication, and caregiving, as well as reduced stress and anxiety levels, the release of oxytocin can also occur in response to negative or stressful situations, such as conflict or trauma, which can influence emotional responses and bonding dynamics in relationships.

Incorporating positive sources of oxytocin into your daily life can foster your emotional well-being. Building and nurturing meaningful relationships, engaging in acts of kindness, and creating a supportive social environment can contribute to a greater sense of bonding and closeness with others. Some positive sources of oxytocin include:

Physical Touch: Hugging, cuddling, holding hands, and other forms of physical touch can stimulate the release of oxytocin. Positive physical contact with loved ones can promote feelings of connection and closeness.

Petting Animals: Interacting with pets, such as petting a dog or cat, can stimulate the release of oxytocin. The companionship and affection of animals can promote feelings of comfort and connection.

Childbirth and Breastfeeding: Oxytocin plays a crucial role during childbirth and breastfeeding, facilitating the mother-infant bond. The physical contact and nurturing involved in caring for a newborn can trigger oxytocin release in both the mother and child.

Dopamine

Dopamine, as previously discussed, plays a role in seeking rewards and experiencing pleasure. It is often referred to as the "feel-good" hormone or neurotransmitter that plays a key role in the brain's reward system and motivation. In abusive relationships, the intermittent reinforcement of affection and abuse can trigger dopamine release, creating a cycle of highs and lows that can be addictive. The release of dopamine during positive experiences can reinforce behaviors that lead to reward and satisfaction, contributing to feelings of attraction, attachment, and happiness in relationships. However, dopamine can also play a role in addictive behaviors and obsessive thinking, leading to an intense focus on the partner or relationship that may not always be healthy or sustainable. The victim may become conditioned to seek out the positive moments with the abuser, even at the cost of enduring the negative ones.

Dopamine levels in the brain can be boosted naturally to promote feelings of pleasure, motivation, and reward. Here are some healthy sources of dopamine:

Exercise: Physical activity, especially aerobic exercise, has been shown to increase dopamine levels in the brain. Engaging in regular exercise can help boost mood and motivation.

Healthy Diet: Foods rich in tyrosine, an amino acid that is a precursor to dopamine, can support dopamine production. Some examples include almonds, avocados, bananas, eggs, and lean proteins like chicken and turkey.

Sleep: Getting an adequate amount of quality sleep is essential for dopamine regulation. Lack of sleep can disrupt dopamine levels and negatively affect mood and motivation.

Sunlight: Sunlight exposure can help increase dopamine production. Spending time outdoors, especially in the morning, can boost mood and energy levels.

Meditation and Mindfulness: Practices like meditation and mindfulness have been shown to increase dopamine levels and improve overall well-being. These techniques can help reduce stress and promote a sense of calm and focus.

Music and Art: Listening to music or engaging in creative activities like painting or drawing can stimulate dopamine release in the brain. Enjoying art and music that you find pleasurable can enhance mood and motivation.

Social Interaction: Positive social interactions, such as spending time with loved ones, laughing, and connecting with others, can also boost dopamine levels. Building strong social connections and engaging in meaningful relationships can promote feelings of happiness and fulfillment.

Incorporating these natural sources of dopamine into your daily routine can help support overall brain health, enhance mood, and increase motivation and reward. It is essential to maintain a healthy lifestyle that includes regular exercise, a balanced diet, sufficient sleep, and positive social interactions to support optimal dopamine function.

Cortisol

Cortisol, known as the "stress hormone" that is released in response to stress, threat, or danger, is often elevated in abusive relationships due to the constant state of fear, anxiety, and uncertainty. The victim's physiological response to the abuse can lead to increased cortisol levels, which can contribute to feelings of powerlessness, hypervigilance, and emotional distress. This heightened stress response can further entrench the victim in the abusive dynamic as the body becomes accustomed to the constant state of arousal and threat. Elevated cortisol levels in response to chronic stress or relationship conflict can have negative effects on physical health, emotional well-being, and relationship satisfaction.

Cortisol can affect communication, emotional regulation, and conflict resolution in relationships, leading to feelings of anxiety, tension, and dysregulation. Effective stress management strategies, communication skills, and emotional support can help regulate cortisol levels and reduce the effects of stress in relationships.

Here are some strategies to help reduce cortisol levels:

Regular Exercise: Physical activity can help reduce cortisol levels and alleviate stress. Engaging in activities like walking, jogging, yoga, or other forms of exercise can promote relaxation and improve mood.

Mindfulness and Meditation: Practices like mindfulness meditation, deep breathing exercises, and progressive muscle relaxation can help lower cortisol levels and promote a sense of calm. Taking time to relax and focus on the present moment can reduce stress and anxiety.

Adequate Sleep: Getting enough quality sleep is crucial for regulating cortisol levels. Establishing a regular sleep routine, creating a calming bedtime ritual, and ensuring a comfortable sleep environment can support restful sleep and lower cortisol levels.

Social Support: Building and maintaining positive social connections can help reduce stress and lower cortisol levels. Spending time with friends and loved ones, sharing feelings, and seeking support when needed can promote emotional well-being.

Relaxation Techniques: Engaging in relaxation techniques, such as progressive muscle relaxation, visualization, or aromatherapy, can help reduce cortisol levels and promote relaxation. Finding activities that help you unwind and de-stress can be beneficial for managing cortisol.

Time in Nature: Spending time outdoors in nature, such as going for a walk in the park or gardening, can help lower cortisol levels and promote relaxation. Connecting with the natural world and enjoying the peaceful surroundings can reduce stress and anxiety.

Incorporating these strategies into your daily routine can help manage cortisol levels, reduce stress, and promote overall well-being. Finding activities that help you relax, unwind, and take care of your physical and emotional health can decrease cortisol levels and improve stress management.

Understanding the roles of oxytocin, dopamine, and cortisol in relationships can provide insights into the neurobiological mechanisms that influence emotional bonding, reward processing, and stress responses in intimate connections. Individuals can replace their hormonal source by fostering positive relationship behaviors, managing stress effectively, and prioritizing emotional well-being through engaging in various physical activities to cultivate healthier and more fulfilling relationships based on trust, communication, and mutual support with friends and family.

2.6 THE EFFECT OF NARCISSISM ON INTIMACY: SEX AND TRUST

Sex can have a profound effect on individuals, especially within the context of a narcissistic relationship. It can blur the lines of intimacy, power dynamics, and control. In the complex realm of interpersonal connections, sex can amplify the intricacies and challenges, particularly when intertwined with narcissistic behavior.

Engaging in sexual encounters with a narcissist can evoke a range of conflicting emotions. The intensity and allure of the experience may heighten the confusion and complexity of the relationship. Narcissists are adept at creating an electric and passionate sexual dynamic, leaving their partners entangled in a web of conflicting feelings.

Some individuals find themselves trapped in a tumultuous relationship where the allure of satisfying sex clashes with the harsh reality of emotional neglect and manipulation. Despite the physical connection being gratifying, the emotional toll of dealing with a callous, unempathetic partner can be overwhelming.

It is crucial not to be deceived by the allure of electrifying sex with a narcissist. The intense sexual experiences are often driven by the narcissist's need for validation and self-gratification rather than genuine care for their partner's well-being.

Narcissists are driven by a desire for admiration and attention, using sex as a tool to feed their egos and fulfill their narcissistic supply.

In a narcissistic dynamic, sex becomes a means of control and manipulation. Narcissists may use sex as a reward for compliance or as a punishment for perceived inadequacies. The hot-and-cold nature of the relationship is further exacerbated by the fluctuating intensity of passion and care, which often diminishes once the sexual encounter concludes.

Ultimately, sex in a narcissistic relationship can be a weapon wielded to assert dominance, manipulate behavior, and fulfill the narcissist's self-serving agenda. As the relationship progresses, the use of sex as a tool for reward or punishment becomes more pronounced, contributing to the volatile and emotionally draining nature of the dynamic.

Narcissistic behaviors pose a significant challenge to the foundations of intimacy and trust in any relationship. The very essence of intimacy - vulnerability and mutual emotional support - is often compromised by the narcissist's inability to empathize and their persistent need to control the relationship dynamics. Narcissists, absorbed in their own needs and feelings, typically struggle to recognize or validate their partner's emotional state. This lack of empathy can manifest as indifference to your emotional needs or an inability to support you during times of stress or sadness. Instead of a partnership that nurtures mutual growth and comfort, the relationship can feel like a one-sided affair where your role is to bolster the narcissist's ego and affirm his/her worth, often at the cost of your emotional well-being.

The control exerted by a narcissist also undermines intimacy. It can be subtle, like making decisions without your input, or more overt, such as criticizing your choices to make you feel incapable of independent thought. Over time, this dynamic fosters an environment of dependency and insecurity. For instance, you might find yourself second-guessing even the simplest decisions that once felt straightforward, such as what to wear to social gatherings, or more significant choices, like career moves, because the narcissist's opinions have overshadowed your own. This erosion of self-confidence is profoundly damaging to intimacy, as true closeness requires both partners to feel valued and capable.

Trust within the relationship suffers under the weight of manipulation and deceit, which are common traits in narcissistic interactions. Narcissists often manipulate facts and situations to their advantage, distorting reality to align with their desires and narratives. This behavior can lead to a profound sense of betrayal for you, as the ground constantly shifts beneath your feet. You may begin to question your reality and doubt your judgment, a state known as gaslighting, which further cements the power imbalance in the relationship. The narcissist might deny events that you remember clearly or react with outrage to discussions about their behavior, insisting that you are the one at fault. This ongoing deceit creates deep-seated trust issues, as you may not only struggle to trust the narcissist but also carry these doubts into other relationships, wary of similar betrayals.

Rebuilding trust and intimacy after experiencing narcissistic abuse involves a deliberate reconnection with your emotional needs and boundaries. Therapy can play a crucial role in this healing journey. A therapist who understands the effect of narcissistic abuse can help you navigate your feelings and begin to separate your self-worth from the approval of the narcissist. A skilled counselor can also guide you in identifying and setting healthy boundaries, which is essential for any future healthy relationship. These boundaries help protect your emotional well-being and create a space where intimacy between partners who respect each other's needs can grow.

Moreover, engaging in activities that reinforce your sense of self can enhance your recovery. This might include pursuits that you had set aside during your relationship with the narcissist, such as hobbies, social activities, or career goals. Reconnecting with these parts of your life can restore your sense of individuality and confidence, which are critical for healthy intimate relationships. As you rebuild your identity, you may find that your capacity for trust and emotional connection strengthens, allowing you to engage more fully and authentically with others.

Self-intimacy is another crucial area to cultivate. This involves developing a deep understanding and acceptance of your emotions and needs. Practices like mindfulness, journaling, and self-compassion exercises can facilitate this connection with yourself. By becoming attuned to your feelings and treating yourself with kindness and understanding, you lay the groundwork for healthier relationships. This self-intimacy ensures that, moving forward, you can recognize and prioritize your emotional needs, discern genuine affection from manipulation, and engage in relationships where mutual trust and intimacy are given freely and reciprocated.

As you navigate the aftermath of a relationship marred by narcissism, remember that the journey back to trust and intimacy is gradual and requires patience with yourself. Each step towards understanding and asserting your emotional needs not only heals the wounds inflicted by narcissistic abuse but also empowers you to establish and maintain the loving, respectful relationships you deserve.

2.7 WHEN CHILDREN ARE INVOLVED: PROTECTING THE VULNERABLE

The presence of children in a relationship complicated by narcissism introduces an additional layer of concern and responsibility. Children, with their inherent emotional sensitivity and dependence, are particularly susceptible to the influences of a narcissistic parent. The effects of such exposure can be far-reaching, potentially shaping their emotional landscape and interpersonal relationships well into adulthood. Narcissists, absorbed in their own needs and devoid of genuine empathy, may use children as tools in their manipulative games, often leaving emotional scars that might not manifest until later in life.

Children raised by narcissistic parents often struggle with issues of self-worth and identity. They may feel that their value is contingent on meeting the narcissistic parent's expectations or providing the parent with a narcissistic supply. This conditional attention can lead to children developing performance-based self-esteem, where they believe they must earn love and approval through achievements or compliance. Such an upbringing can instill deep-seated fears of rejection and a pervasive sense of inadequacy, which might hinder their ability to form healthy relationships. Furthermore, children may mimic the narcissistic behaviors modeled by the parent, such as manipulation and lack of empathy, and adopt these traits, believing that they are necessary for relationship success.

Protecting children from the detrimental effects of a narcissistic parent is crucial yet challenging. One effective strategy involves the other parent providing a consistent and contrasting example of empathy, respect, and unconditional love. By actively demonstrating healthy emotional responses and interactions, the non-narcissistic parent can counterbalance narcissistic behaviors, giving the child a broader perspective on personal relationships and self-worth. It is also important to engage in open and age-appropriate conversations with children about emotions and relationships, helping them understand and label their experiences accurately. This can empower children to recognize unhealthy behaviors and differentiate them from normal relational dynamics.

Creating a safe emotional space for children to express their feelings is another protective strategy. This involves acknowledging and validating their emotions without judgment, providing reassurance, and encouraging open communication. Such an environment can help mitigate the confusion and self-doubt instilled by the narcissistic parent, fostering a stronger sense of self and emotional resilience in the child.

Legal Considerations and Protective Measures

Navigating the legal landscape in the context of a narcissistic relationship requires careful consideration, especially when children are involved. Legal measures can provide a framework for protecting the children's physical and emotional well-being. Custody arrangements that limit the narcissistic parent's potential for emotional manipulation are crucial. This might involve supervised visitation or guidelines for communication between the narcissistic parent and the child, ensuring any interaction does not undermine the child's emotional health.

Documenting instances of manipulative or harmful behavior by the narcissist can be an essential part of legal strategy. Keeping a detailed record of interactions that highlight the narcissist's parenting deficiencies can support custody and visitation arguments in court. It is advisable to work closely with legal professionals who understand the nuances of narcissistic behavior and can advocate effectively for the children's best interests.

Support Systems and Resources

Establishing a robust support system is vital for both the children and the custodial parent. Professional counseling can play a significant role in addressing the psychological effects of living with a narcissistic parent. Child psychologists or therapists trained in dealing with emotional abuse are equipped to help children unpack their experiences and develop healthier emotional and relational patterns.

Support groups for survivors of narcissistic relationships can also provide both peer support and practical advice for dealing with the complexities of co-parenting with a narcissist. These groups comprise individuals who understand the unique challenges involved and can offer empathy and support.

Additionally, educational resources about narcissism and its effects on families can be invaluable. Books, workshops, and online platforms dedicated to this subject can provide insights and strategies for coping with the challenges posed by narcissistic relationships. These resources not only educate but also validate the experiences of those dealing with narcissists, which is crucial for overcoming the isolation and gaslighting often experienced in these relationships.

As this chapter concludes, it is important to recognize the profound effects of a narcissistic parent on children and the broader family dynamics. The strategies and considerations outlined here aim to protect the most vulnerable and foster an environment where healing and healthy relational patterns can flourish. Moving forward, the next chapter delves into the strategies needed to deal with a narcissist in various contexts, providing further guidance on navigating these complex interactions.

CHAPTER 3
LIVING WITH A
NARCISSIST

Navigating life with a narcissist can often feel like walking through a meticulously crafted maze, where each turn is designed to disorient and confuse, leaving you questioning your sense of reality and self-worth. This chapter aims to equip you with a compass in the form of boundary-setting techniques, a tool indispensable for maintaining your autonomy and safeguarding your self-esteem in the unpredictable terrain of a narcissistic relationship.

By setting, communicating, and consistently enforcing these boundaries, you reclaim control over your own life, reducing the chaos that so often accompanies relationships with narcissists.

3.1 SETTING BOUNDARIES: TECHNIQUES THAT WORK WITH A NARCISSIST

Understanding the Importance of Boundaries

Boundaries are your lines in the sand, the limits you set to protect your well-being in any relationship. When dealing with a narcissist, boundaries become your armor. Narcissists, known for their manipulative and often invasive behaviors, respect neither space nor limits, viewing them as challenges to their authority and control. By setting and enforcing robust boundaries, you assert your independence and demand respect, two elements narcissists often strive to suppress. These boundaries help delineate a clear line between acceptable and unacceptable behaviors, effectively communicating to the narcissist that their typical manipulations and encroachments will not be tolerated. It is a crucial step in mitigating the psychological toll of such relationships, ensuring that your values and needs are recognized and respected.

Techniques for Effective Boundary-Setting

Setting boundaries with narcissists is not about changing their behaviors but rather about changing your response to their actions. The first step is to define what you are and are not willing to tolerate. Be specific and realistic about what behaviors you can and cannot accept. For instance, you might decide that you will no longer engage in conversations where you are belittled or gaslighted.

Once your boundaries are defined, communicate them clearly and assertively to the narcissist. This communication does not need to be confrontational but should be firm and devoid of ambiguity. A statement like, "I need our discussions to remain respectful, and I will remove myself from the conversation if it becomes demeaning," sets a clear expectation and outlines the consequence for crossing that boundary.

Visualizing a glass wall between yourself and an abuser can be a powerful metaphor for setting boundaries and protecting yourself from harm. It empowers you to assert your own needs, establish limits on what you will tolerate, and prioritize your well-being in the face of abuse.

The glass wall acts as a physical barrier that prevents the abuser from getting too close or causing harm. It creates a safe space for you to retreat to when you feel threatened or overwhelmed by the abuser's behavior.

By visualizing a glass wall between yourself and the abuser, you can gain clarity and perspective on the situation. It helps you see the dynamics of the relationship more clearly and recognize the unhealthy behaviors and patterns at play.

The glass wall also serves as an emotional barrier, shielding you from the negative energy, manipulation, and toxicity of the abuser. It allows you to maintain a sense of inner peace and emotional well-being in the face of abuse. The wall can also reinforce your inner strength and resilience. It reminds you that you have the power to protect yourself, stand up for your rights, and break free from the cycle of abuse.

You are taking back control over your own life and asserting your autonomy in the face of the abuser's attempts to exert power and control over you. It empowers you to make choices that are in your best interests and aligned with your values and beliefs.

Enforcing these boundaries is perhaps the most challenging step, as it requires consistency. Every time a boundary is violated, follow through with the consequence you have communicated. This might mean ending a conversation abruptly or stepping away from a situation until it can be approached with respect. The narcissist must see that your boundaries are not negotiable and that your measures are serious and not merely threats.

Handling Boundary Violations

Despite your best efforts, narcissists will inevitably violate your boundaries. They test limits as a form of control and to gauge your resolve. When a boundary is crossed, address it immediately. Delayed consequences can send mixed signals, diminishing the effectiveness of your boundaries.

Remain calm and assertive in your responses. Avoid getting drawn into arguments and emotional manipulation. Reinforce your boundary by restating it and following through with the established consequence.

In situations where boundary violations become repetitive or increasingly severe, consider seeking external support.

A therapist, particularly one experienced in dealing with narcissistic behaviors, can provide you with the strategies.

Clearly communicate consequences for continued boundary violations. Let the narcissist know what will happen if he/she continues to disregard your boundaries, and be prepared to follow through with those consequences if necessary.

If the narcissist continues to violate your boundaries despite your attempts to communicate and set limits, consider limiting or cutting off contact with him/her.

Protecting yourself from further harm is important, and sometimes, creating physical or emotional distance is necessary.

Maintaining Consistency

The effectiveness of boundaries lies in their consistent enforcement. Narcissists are adept at detecting and exploiting any signs of wavering resolve, and inconsistent boundary enforcement can encourage further transgressions. It is essential to remain vigilant and steadfast, regardless of the emotional or psychological tactics a narcissist might employ.

To aid in maintaining consistency, keep a journal of interactions, noting when and how boundaries were tested and the response these actions elicited. This record can serve not only as a reminder of the necessity of your boundaries but also as a reinforcement of your commitment to uphold them. Additionally, cultivate a support network of friends, family, or professionals who understand your situation and can offer encouragement and advice when maintaining boundaries becomes challenging.

When living with a narcissist, boundaries are not just lines drawn in self-defense; they are declarations of self-respect and indicators of your strength. This proactive stance empowers you to interact on your terms, fostering a sense of security and respect that narcissistic dynamics often seek to undermine. Through these steps, you fortify your psychological and emotional defenses, ensuring that your interactions are governed by mutual respect and recognition not dominated by manipulation and disrespect.

3.2 COMMUNICATING UNDER PRESSURE: STRATEGIES FOR EVERYDAY INTERACTIONS

When engaged in daily interactions with a narcissist, maintaining your composure can often feel like trying to stay calm in the eye of a storm. The key to navigating these turbulent waters lies not only in your response at the moment but also in your preparation and mindset beforehand. Techniques such as deep breathing and staying focused on the facts can serve as anchors, preventing you from being swept away by emotional currents. Deep breathing, for instance, is not just about taking slow breaths; it is a method to center yourself to return to a state of calm from where you can think and communicate more clearly. Before starting a conversation with a narcissist, take a few moments to breathe deeply, focusing solely on the air entering and leaving your body to ground yourself in the present moment.

Staying focused on the facts is equally crucial. Narcissists often employ tactics such as gaslighting or shifting the topic to disorient you and gain the upper hand. By maintaining a sharp focus on the topic at hand and not getting sidetracked by the narcissist's attempts to distract or confuse, you can keep the conversation on track. Prepare by clearly knowing the points you want to discuss and sticking to them, regardless of the provocations or manipulations that might arise. If the interaction begins to veer off course, gently steer it back to the main issue, repeating your points as necessary to keep the discussion anchored.

Choosing your battles wisely is another vital strategy in dealing with a narcissist. Not every issue needs to be addressed, and recognizing which battles are worth your energy is crucial for preserving your mental health. Some conflicts, particularly those that challenge your core values or boundaries, may necessitate a firm stance, while others might be more effectively handled by agreeing to disagree or even letting them go entirely. This selective engagement prevents unnecessary conflicts and conserves your energy to focus on more significant issues. It is about assessing the potential effects of the issue at hand - will this matter in the long term, or can it be overlooked for the sake of peace?

Assertive communication is your strongest tool in clearly expressing your needs and expectations without aggression or passivity. Using "I" statements is a great way to voice your thoughts and feelings without sounding accusatory, which can escalate tensions. For example, instead of saying, "You never listen to me," try, "I feel unheard when I speak and would appreciate it if you could pay closer attention." This method communicates your feelings and desires directly and respectfully without casting blame. It is essential to practice this style of communication consistently, as it promotes a healthier dialogue and sets a tone of mutual respect.

Avoiding common communication traps such as JADE (Justify, Argue, Defend, Explain) is crucial when dealing with a narcissist. Engaging in these behaviors often leads to circular arguments with no resolution, draining your energy and leaving you feeling frustrated and defeated.

Narcissists thrive on the chaos and confusion that such exchanges provoke, and by refusing to participate in these patterns, you deprive them of the reaction they seek.

When you feel pulled into justifying your actions or decisions, pause and remind yourself that you do not owe excessive explanations for your boundaries or choices. If the conversation becomes an argument with no clear endpoint, it might be more prudent to disengage and revisit the discussion later when both parties are calmer.

By employing these strategies, you can navigate interactions with a narcissist more effectively, maintaining your dignity and peace of mind. Remember, the goal is not to change the narcissist's behavior - that is beyond your control - but to manage how you respond, conserving your emotional resources and ensuring your voice is heard and respected.

3.3 MANAGING NARCISSISTIC RAGE AND EMOTIONAL OUTBURSTS

Understanding the triggers and early signs of narcissistic rage can significantly alter the dynamics of your interactions with a narcissist. This type of rage, often explosive and unpredictable, stems not from a typical emotional reaction but rather from a deep-seated need to assert dominance and control. Recognizing the precursors to these emotional outbursts can provide critical insights that enable you to de-escalate potential conflicts before they escalate into full-blown confrontations. Common signs that narcissists might be on the brink of a rage episode include their tone of voice becoming more critical, body language that may seem tense or aggressive, and a pattern of interrupting or talking over you to reassert their dominance. They may also exhibit signs of paranoia or become excessively defensive over seemingly minor issues. These indicators, often subtle, signal an internal struggle with perceived threats to their ego or authority.

When you notice these warning signs, it is crucial to implement de-escalation techniques swiftly. One effective strategy is distraction, which involves shifting the conversation away from the topic that is triggering the narcissist's defensive stance. This could be as simple as introducing an unrelated topic or activity that can diffuse the building tension. For instance, if a discussion about weekend plans begins to heat up, you might pivot to discussing a new restaurant or movie you heard about. The key is to redirect the narcissist's attention to something less charged, reducing the immediacy of his/her emotional reaction. Knowing when to exit the conversation is another critical technique. If the narcissist's behavior escalates to the point at which distraction becomes ineffective, it may be necessary to remove yourself from the situation. This is not about conceding defeat but rather about protecting your emotional well-being. Politely excusing yourself with a statement like, "I can see this topic is causing tension; perhaps we can revisit it another time when things are calmer," can prevent the situation from escalating further and give both parties time to cool down.

Protecting yourself during these outbursts is paramount. Physical safety should always be a priority, and if at any point you feel threatened, it is important to leave the environment immediately. Emotional protection is equally crucial. One technique is emotional detachment, which involves maintaining an internal distance from the emotional chaos by reminding yourself that the narcissist's outbursts are not a reflection of your worth but rather indicative of his/her internal struggles. Visualizing an emotional shield can also be helpful, imagining a barrier that protects you from the negative energy of the narcissist's words or actions. This visualization reinforces your position as an observer rather than a participant in the outburst, which can help maintain your emotional equilibrium.

Post-outburst management focuses on recovery and setting the stage for future interactions. After an episode of narcissistic rage, it is essential to engage in self-care practices that restore your sense of calm and equilibrium. This might involve activities that you find soothing, such as reading, walking, or meditating. It is also important to assess the interaction and prepare for future encounters, which might mean setting stricter boundaries or having a quick exit plan in similar situations.

Additionally, when interactions resume, clearly communicate that respectful behavior is mandatory for any further engagement. This sets a precedent that emotional outbursts do not lead to the desired outcome and that calm, respectful communication is the only way forward. Through these strategies, you can manage the immediate challenges of narcissistic rage and contribute to a healthier interaction dynamic over time, ensuring your emotional needs are met and your boundaries are respected.

3.4 WHEN LEAVING IS NOT AN OPTION: COPING MECHANISMS FOR LONG-TERM EXPOSURE

In situations where extricating oneself from a relationship with a narcissist is not feasible due to financial, familial, or personal reasons, developing strategies to mitigate the effects of the narcissist's behavior becomes crucial. Building emotional resilience, in this context, is not merely about enduring but rather about cultivating an inner strength that preserves your sense of self and enhances your ability to deal with stress. Emotional resilience can be envisioned as a muscle that can be strengthened with practice and patience. It involves a blend of self-awareness, mindfulness, and active engagement in practices that foster emotional stability and growth.

To start building this resilience, begin with mindfulness practices that center your thoughts and feelings in the present moment, reducing the effects of the narcissist's attempts to destabilize your emotional world. Techniques such as focused breathing, meditation, or yoga can serve as daily touchstones that help you regain a sense of self-control and peace. Incorporating these practices into your routine can help anchor you in your own experiences and emotions, making it harder for the narcissist to knock you off balance. Moreover, mindfulness encourages a reflective rather than reactive approach to interactions, which is crucial in dealing with a narcissist's provocations.

Self-awareness is another key component of emotional resilience. This involves understanding your emotional triggers and the effects of the narcissist's behaviors on you. Keeping a journal can be a transformative practice in this regard. Document your interactions with the narcissist and reflect on them. Which comments or behaviors triggered a strong emotional response? Why? Understanding these patterns can help you anticipate and neutralize potential triggers in future interactions, thereby maintaining your emotional equilibrium.

The importance of a robust support network cannot be overstated when living with a narcissist. Social support provides not only an emotional lifeline but also alternative perspectives that can help counteract the distortion of reality that often comes with narcissistic manipulation. Building this network might involve reaching out to old friends or making new ones, joining support groups, or engaging in community activities. These connections can provide emotional validation and reinforcement of your experiences, countering the isolation that narcissists often foster around their partners.

Finding a therapist experienced in dealing with narcissistic relationships can also be invaluable. Therapy offers a safe space to explore the feelings and challenges of living with a narcissist, providing professional insights into managing these dynamics. Therapists can also help set realistic goals for the relationship, guiding you in managing your expectations and developing coping strategies tailored to your specific situation.

Engaging in activities outside of the relationship that provide fulfillment and distraction is essential for maintaining your well-being. Whether it is a hobby, sport, or creative endeavor, these activities offer an outlet for stress and a means for building a positive self-identity independent of the relationship. They remind you of your capabilities and worth outside of the narcissist's shadow, reinforcing your sense of self and providing a necessary counterbalance to the relationship's dynamics.

Setting realistic expectations about the relationship and the narcissist is crucial for your mental and emotional health. This involves accepting that the narcissist may never fully recognize or meet your emotional needs. Adjusting your expectations helps reduce daily frustrations and disappointments. It is about acknowledging the limitations of the narcissist's capacity to change and focusing instead on ways to enrich your own life and happiness. This adjustment is not about lowering your standards but about redirecting your energy toward realistically changeable and fulfilling matters.

These strategies, collectively aimed at building emotional resilience, enhancing social support, and maintaining personal fulfillment, form a comprehensive approach to managing life with a narcissist when separation is not an option. They emphasize the importance of self-care and personal growth, ensuring that your life remains rich and meaningful, irrespective of the challenges posed by the narcissistic relationship. Engaging actively with these practices can transform the narrative from mere survival to thriving despite the complexities of your circumstances.

3.5 THE ROLE OF SELF-CARE: KEEPING YOUR SANITY INTACT

Self-care is not just a buzzword; it is an essential strategy for maintaining your sanity and well-being, especially when navigating the turbulent waters of life with a narcissist. When you are constantly exposed to the stress that comes with such a relationship, it is crucial to have a robust self-care routine that covers various aspects of your health—emotional, physical, spiritual, and social. These practices help fortify your resilience against the psychological wear and tear that can arise from ongoing emotional challenges.

Fundamentals of Self-Care

The foundation of effective self-care is understanding that your needs are valid and important, deserving attention and respect. This encompasses various practices that keep you grounded and balanced. Setting aside time for yourself to breathe and reflect away from the chaos that might engulf your home environment is crucial, even if it is just a few minutes each day. This time should be non-negotiable, a sanctuary where the focus is solely on your well-being. It is also beneficial to cultivate a routine that includes activities that you love and that connect you back to yourself, be it reading, walking, or any other hobby that brings you joy and peace. These moments of pleasure are vital for maintaining your emotional health and reminding you of your worth outside of your relationship dynamics.

Emotional Self-Care Techniques

Journaling stands out as a particularly effective tool for emotional self-care. It serves as a safe space to express your thoughts and feelings, process your experiences, and gain clarity. The act of writing can be therapeutic, helping you externalize what you are going through and often providing a new perspective on the situation. Similarly, engaging in mindfulness practices, such as meditation, can significantly alleviate stress. These practices encourage you to stay present and focused, reducing anxiety and helping you manage your reactions to the narcissist's behaviors. For those who find solace in creativity, art and music can be powerful outlets for expression and healing. Creating something new can be incredibly empowering, offering a sense of accomplishment and a break from negative emotional cycles.

Physical Self-Care Routines

Physical health is often one of the first casualties in a stressful environment.

Regular physical activity, sufficient sleep, and proper nutrition are pivotal for maintaining your strength and health, which in turn support your emotional and mental resilience.

Exercise, whether it is yoga, running, or dancing, not only improves your physical health but also releases endorphins that can boost your mood and counteract the depressive effects of stress. Prioritizing sleep is equally important.

Preventing you from sleep or disturbing your sleep is one of the manipulative tactics employed by narcissists to create emotional distress.

A lack of rest can impair your judgment, make you more susceptible to stress, and decrease your overall emotional resilience.

Nutrition also plays a critical role; nourishing your body with the right foods can stabilize your mood, improve your energy levels, and enhance your ability to cope with stress.

Spiritual and Social Self-Care

For many, spiritual practices - whether they involve organized religion, meditation, nature walks, or other forms of spiritual expression - provide a significant source of comfort and perspective. These practices can offer a sense of connection to something greater than oneself, which can be particularly grounding in times of turmoil. Maintaining social connections is also a critical component of self-care. Relationships with friends, family, or supportive communities provide emotional sustenance and a reminder that you are not alone. These connections can offer both practical and emotional support, providing a buffer against the isolation that often comes from relationships with narcissists.

Incorporating these self-care practices into your daily life can create a robust buffer against the negative effects of living with a narcissist. Each aspect of self-care supports the others, creating a comprehensive care system that sustains your physical, mental, emotional, and spiritual well-being. Through dedicated self-care, you ensure that you are the best version of yourself, capable of facing the challenges that arise with strength, clarity, and resilience.

3.6 LEGAL AND FINANCIAL CONSIDERATIONS IN A NARCISSISTIC PARTNERSHIP

Understanding your legal rights and preparing financially are critical steps when navigating a partnership with a narcissist, particularly when contemplating separation or divorce.

Financial and legal entanglements can be complex and fraught with manipulation, making it essential to approach these aspects with careful planning and informed strategies.

Understanding Legal Rights

Awareness of your legal rights, especially regarding property, custody of children, and financial entitlements, is crucial when in a relationship with a narcissist.

Laws vary significantly by location, so it is imperative to familiarize yourself with the regulations in your area.

This knowledge provides a strong foundation for protecting your interests, particularly in a divorce or separation scenario where a narcissist may attempt to leverage legal processes to their advantage.

For instance, understanding marital property laws can help you make informed decisions about how to divide assets fairly despite your partner's attempts to obscure or devalue your contributions. Similarly, knowing your rights concerning child custody and support can protect you against your narcissist partner's attempts to use children as leverage.

Consulting with a legal professional who has experience dealing with high-conflict personalities can prove invaluable. This professional can guide you through the complexities of your specific situation and help ensure that your rights are fully protected.

This includes navigating the intricacies of custody arrangements and ensuring that financial settlements are equitable, considering the unique dynamics in relationships involving narcissism.

Preparing Financially

Financial preparation is another crucial area requiring attention. Narcissists often exert control through financial means, making financial independence a critical step towards autonomy. Begin by securing personal finances, which includes setting up individual bank accounts and establishing credit in your name. It is especially important if you have shared accounts or if your credit is intertwined with your partner's.

Gathering and organizing all financial documents, including bank statements, tax returns, and any documentation about shared assets or debts, is a necessary step. Having a clear picture of both your and your partner's financial situation helps prevent

any surprises during legal proceedings and supports fair nego-
tiations.

Developing a budget based on your projected income and neces-
sities post-separation can also empower you to make informed
decisions and plan for a future independent of financial manipulation. Consider consulting with a financial advisor to help navigate this transition, ensuring you can sustain your living
standards and meet any obligations during and after the separation process.

Navigating Divorce or Separation

Divorcing a narcissist involves unique challenges, as narcissists
often use the legal process to continue their patterns of control
and manipulation. Choosing the right lawyer is crucial; someone
experienced in dealing with high-conflict divorce cases and
knowledgeable about narcissistic behaviors can be a significant
asset. They can strategize effectively to mitigate the narcissist's
tactics and help expedite the proceedings in a manner that minimizes stress and conflict.

Preparing for potential legal manipulations by the narcissist, such
as delaying tactics or false accusations, is also essential. Your
lawyer can help anticipate these moves and prepare countermeasures, ensuring that the process stays on track and your interests
are protected. Documenting all interactions with the narcissist
can provide crucial evidence to support your case, underscoring
the necessity of your claims and countering any misinformation
the narcissist might present.

Protecting Assets and Future Security

Finally, protecting your assets and securing your financial future is paramount. Legal measures, such as prenuptial agreements or, in the absence of one, clear documentation of asset ownership, can be crucial. During the divorce, ensure all assets are accounted for and properly valued, preventing the narcissist from hiding or undervaluing what is rightfully part of the marital estate.

After the separation, shifting your financial focus towards rebuilding and securing your economic stability is vital. This step might include revising your will, changing beneficiaries on insurance policies and retirement accounts, and ensuring your assets are protected from any future claims by the narcissist. Investments in your name alone, secure savings strategies, and continuous monitoring of your credit report can further safeguard your financial independence.

Navigating a relationship with a narcissist involves not just emotional but considerable legal and financial considerations. By understanding your rights, preparing financially, strategically navigating the separation process, and safeguarding your assets, you can establish a foundation for a stable and secure future free of manipulation. This preparation not only protects you but also empowers you to move forward with confidence as you close this challenging chapter of your life.

As this chapter concludes, the focus on legal and financial strategies underscores the broader themes of empowerment and self-preservation that are crucial when dealing with a narcissist. The subsequent chapters build on these foundations, exploring further how to reclaim your life and thrive post-narcissism.

CHAPTER 4

BREAKING FREE AND HEALING

Navigating through the fog of a relationship tainted by narcissism often leaves you questioning not only the intentions of your partner but also the essence of your reality. It is a journey marked by confusion, turmoil, and profound self-doubt. However, amidst this chaos comes a pivotal moment - a clear albeit difficult realization that the path you are on is unsustainable. This chapter is dedicated to recognizing this critical juncture when the scales have tipped irrevocably, necessitating the departure for the sake of your own mental and physical well-being.

4.1 RECOGNIZING THE EXIT SIGNS: WHEN IT IS TIME TO LEAVE

Identifying Deal-Breakers

In every relationship marred by narcissism, specific behaviors and situations should be recognized as deal-breakers. These are not just the occasional disagreements or challenging days that couples universally face but rather profound betrayals of respect and patterns of manipulation that cut to the very core of one's dignity. For instance, you might find that your achievements are consistently minimized or ridiculed, your feelings are regularly dismissed or belittled, or infidelity is excused under the guise of your supposed inadequacies. These actions are not mere oversights; rather, they indicate a deeper disregard for your worth as an individual. Recognizing these signs is not about nitpicking every fault but about discerning when certain lines, which you deem crucial for your self-respect and emotional health, have been crossed.

Assessing Personal Limits

Understanding and asserting your limits is crucial. It involves a deep introspection to define what you can tolerate and where you draw the line. This boundary-setting is deeply personal and can vary widely from one individual to another. What is intolerable to one might be acceptable to another.

However, the key lies in honesty with oneself, in recognizing the point at which the relationship no longer adds value to your life but instead consistently detracts from your well-being. Engaging in this reflective process is not an admission of defeat but an act of self-preservation. It demands courage to look inward and acknowledge that your limits have been not just tested but exhausted.

Effects on Health and Well-Being

The realization that a narcissistic relationship takes a great toll on your health precedes the decision to leave. Long-term exposure to narcissistic abuse can lead to a spectrum of psychological and physical symptoms. Anxiety, depression, chronic stress, and a lowered immune response are not uncommon.

The constant state of alertness, feeling as if walking on eggshells, can leave you emotionally and physically drained - a shell of your former self. In such cases, leaving becomes more than a choice; it becomes a necessity for recovery.

Understanding this causal link between your relationship and your health issues can often be the catalyst needed to propel you toward the decision to leave.

Psychosomatic Symptoms and Diseases to Be Aware of

Victims of narcissistic abuse experience a range of psychosomatic symptoms and diseases caused by mental or emotional factors, such as stress, anxiety, or trauma. Chronic tension headaches or migraines triggered by stress and emotional turmoil are among the most common side effects.

Other conditions include irritable bowel syndrome (IBS), indigestion, stomach ulcers, generalized body aches, and muscle tension.

Feeling constantly tired or lacking energy is also a result of the emotional rollercoaster. Stress and anxiety can trigger or worsen skin conditions like eczema, psoriasis, or acne.

The constant emotional manipulation, gaslighting, and unpredictability in a narcissistic relationship can contribute to anxiety and depression.

Constant stress and turmoil can indeed lead to hormonal imbalances and infertility in women. When the body is under stress for extended periods, it can disrupt the balance of cortisol, estrogen, progesterone, and other hormones, leading to various health issues, such as irregular menstrual cycles, fertility problems, mood swings, weight gain, and even an increased risk of conditions, like polycystic ovary syndrome (PCOS) or adrenal fatigue.

Chronic stress can affect blood sugar levels and insulin sensitivity in various ways, potentially leading to an increased risk of developing type 2 diabetes or exacerbating symptoms in those already diagnosed with diabetes.

When a person is under stress, the body releases stress hormones like cortisol and adrenaline, which can cause blood sugar levels to rise. Over time, this can strain the body's insulin response and lead to insulin resistance, a key factor in the development of type 2 diabetes.

Furthermore, stress can also influence behaviors that affect diabetes risk, such as overeating, poor food choices, lack of physical activity, and disrupted sleep patterns.

These factors can further contribute to the development or progression of diabetes in individuals under chronic stress.

Long-term exposure to stress in a toxic relationship contributes to high blood pressure, heart palpitations, or other cardiovascular problems.

Though the relationship between stress and cancer is complex and not fully understood, many specialists believe that chronic stress can weaken the immune system, increase inflammation in the body, and affect various physiological functions, which in turn may play a role in cancer development.

While stress itself does not directly cause cancer, it can affect the body in ways that may contribute to the development or progression of cancer.

Stress can also lead to the adoption of unhealthy coping mechanisms, such as smoking, excessive drinking, poor diet, and lack of exercise, all of which are known risk factors for cancer.

Additionally, stress can affect hormone levels (as mentioned earlier), which may influence the growth of certain types of hormone-sensitive cancers.

Stress management is crucial for overall health and well-being. It is important to recognize these effects and seek help to heal from the emotional wounds inflicted by a narcissistic relationship.

Therapy, support groups, self-care practices, and setting boundaries are all essential steps in the healing process.

Remember that you deserve to be in a healthy and supportive relationship where your well-being is valued and respected.

Listening to Instinct and Advice

In the throes of a relationship with a narcissist, your inner voice is often drowned out by the cacophony of manipulation and criticism. Reconnecting with and trusting your instincts can be a significant step in recognizing when it is time to leave. Often, your gut feelings are the first to alert you of danger, to tell you that something is profoundly wrong. Listening to these instincts is crucial.

If you disregard those instincts, your body will send you alerts. Ignoring important symptoms, such as headaches, sleep disturbances, changes in appetite, and increased heart rate, can further lead to all the physical and psychosomatic illnesses mentioned above.

Turning to trusted friends, family members, or professionals who can provide an objective perspective on your relationship can help affirm your feelings. These external viewpoints can serve as crucial support, helping you trust your perceptions and reinforcing the decision to leave for your safety and well-being.

Navigating the decision to leave a narcissistic relationship is undeniably complex and fraught with emotional turmoil. However, recognizing the signs that it is time to move on is a crucial step toward reclaiming your life and embarking on a path to healing. As you reflect on these indicators - deal-breakers, personal limits, health effects, and the advice of trusted others - you equip yourself with the knowledge and courage needed to step away from the destructive cycle of narcissistic abuse and lead a healthier, more fulfilling life.

4.2 PLANNING YOUR EXIT: SAFE AND STRATEGIC APPROACHES

When the decision to leave a narcissistic relationship becomes imminent, the execution of that decision becomes paramount. Crafting a detailed exit plan is akin to drawing a map in uncharted territory; it requires meticulous attention to both the broad strokes and finer details. Devising a financial preparedness plan, securing suitable housing, and addressing legal matters form the scaffold of your strategy. It involves gathering important documents - such as your ID, bank statements, and any legal papers - and placing them into a secure location the narcissist cannot access. Financial preparation extends beyond mere accumulation of funds; it encompasses opening new bank accounts in your name only and rerouting your paycheck if necessary. Secure, alternate housing is crucial, as it provides not only physical but also emotional distance from the narcissist. Whether it is renting a new apartment or arranging to stay with a friend, ensure this sanctuary is lined up well before you disclose your plans to leave, if you disclose them at all.

The shadow of potential backlash from the narcissist looms large in the planning phase. Protecting yourself against this requires preemptive and ongoing safety measures. Change passwords and enhance security on all electronic devices and online accounts to prevent unauthorized access. If there is a history of physical threats, local law enforcement should be alerted about your situation; sometimes, a restraining order may be necessary. In circumstances where children are involved, their safety and emotional well-being must also be prioritized, with steps taken to ensure their transition is handled with sensitivity and care, keeping their routines as uninterrupted as possible.

Securing Confidential Support

Amidst these logistical arrangements, building a covert support network is essential. This network should ideally include legal and therapeutic professionals experienced in dealing with high-conflict separations. Lawyers can provide guidance on the best legal strategies and help you understand your rights, particularly regarding custody and division of assets. Therapists or counselors specializing in narcissistic abuse recovery can offer not just emotional support but also practical advice on navigating the complex feelings that accompany leaving a narcissist. This support network must be established discreetly to prevent the narcissist from undermining your plans or retaliating in harmful ways. For instance, use a new email account to communicate with your lawyer or therapist, and avoid shared computers or devices that the narcissist could access.

The timing and logistics of your departure are critical components of your exit plan. Timing your leave involves a strategic calculation, considering factors such as financial readiness, legal advice, and emotional preparedness. It might coincide with a certain event, like the narcissist being away on a business trip, which can provide the necessary window to move your belongings and start anew without immediate confrontation. The logistics should be organized with precision, from packing your essentials to arranging transportation. If possible, enlist a trusted friend to assist you on the day of the departure to provide emotional support and ensure the process proceeds as planned. The goal is to minimize conflict and avoid tipping off the narcissist until you are safely and securely relocated.

In this meticulously planned departure, while every detail counts, so does the recognition of your courage. Leaving a narcissist is not merely an act of defiance but a profound step towards reclaiming your life and your identity. The road ahead will undoubtedly have its challenges, but the strategic planning you undertake now lays the groundwork for a future defined not by manipulation and control but by freedom and renewal.

4.3 LIFE AFTER NARCISSISM: REBUILDING SELF-CONFIDENCE AND TRUST

After stepping away from the shadow of a narcissistic relationship, you find yourself at a critical crossroad - a point where the journey of self-reconstruction begins. It is akin to revisiting the essence of who you were before the relationship while also discovering new facets of your identity that were previously unexplored or suppressed. This process is not just about recovery; it is about a renaissance of the self, an opportunity to redefine your identity and interests in ways that resonate more deeply with your true self.

From my observations, many individuals choose to stay alone after relationships with narcissists. It is common for individuals to need time to heal from the emotional wounds and psychological trauma caused by abuse. Staying alone allows them to focus on self-care, self-reflection, and personal growth without the distractions and potential harm of another relationship. It takes time to establish healthy boundaries and learn to assert your needs and preferences.

The trauma and pain caused by a relationship with a narcissist can leave lasting scars and a fear of being hurt again. Staying alone may provide a sense of safety and protection from the risk of entering another harmful relationship.

Some women may choose to stay alone to break the cycle of toxic relationships and avoid repeating the patterns of abuse they experienced with a narcissist. Taking time to reflect on past dynamics and understand unhealthy relationship patterns can help make healthier choices in the future.

Restoring One's Self-Identity

The task of rediscovering and reaffirming one's identity post-narcissism involves peeling back the layers of influence and manipulation that may have reshaped how you see yourself. It is common to emerge from such relationships with a distorted sense of self, having had your preferences, desires, and even your perceptions continually undermined. To begin the process of restoration, start by reconnecting with your interests and activities that brought you joy and fulfillment before or outside of the relationship. This could be as simple as restarting an old hobby, like painting or hiking, or as significant as returning to a career path or educational pursuit that was set aside. Engage in these activities without judgment, allowing yourself the freedom to explore what genuinely makes you happy.

Additionally, consider therapy or counseling as a safe space to unpack the remnants of the relationship. A professional can help you work through any residual feelings of guilt, inadequacy, or dependency that the narcissist may have instilled and assist in rebuilding your self-esteem, offering tools and strategies to affirm your worth and capabilities. This therapeutic journey can often lead to profound insights into personal values and goals, facilitating a stronger and more defined sense of self that is aligned with your true aspirations and ideals.

Building Independence

Achieving independence after a narcissistic relationship encompasses several dimensions—financial, emotional, and social. Financial independence is crucial and can be one of the more daunting aspects to tackle, especially if the relationship involves financial control or dependency. Begin by assessing your current financial status, including any debts or assets that are in your name. Creating a budget to meet your basic needs and saving goals is a practical step towards stability. If employment is an issue, start by updating your resume or seeking skills training in your field of interest. The goal is to establish a financial foundation that supports your independence and future growth.

Emotionally, independence is about learning to validate your feelings and decisions without external approval. This can be challenging, particularly if your relationship involves constant belittling or questioning of your judgment. Strengthening your decision-making skills can start with small, everyday choices, gradually building up to more significant life decisions. Each step reinforces your capability and autonomy, slowly diminishing the lingering effects of the narcissist's influence.

Socially, independence involves re-establishing old connections or forming new ones that affirm your worth and respect your boundaries. It might require stepping out of your comfort zone, joining clubs or groups that align with your interests, or volunteering. Each social interaction is an opportunity to reinforce your sense of self and your ability to interact authentically with others.

Setting New Personal Goals

Setting new personal goals post-narcissism is not just about moving forward; it is about reclaiming your future. Start by envisioning where you see yourself personally and professionally in the next few years. Setting specific, measurable, achievable, relevant, and time-bound (SMART) goals can provide clear benchmarks for success and a roadmap to achieving your dreams. Whether it is pursuing a new career, buying a home, or achieving a personal milestone, like running a marathon, these goals should reflect your true aspirations, free from the narcissist's shadow.

Engaging in New Relationships

Entering new relationships after experiencing narcissistic abuse requires caution and a renewed sense of what healthy dynamics look like. Building trust gradually as you learn more about the other person is important. Pay attention to red flags, such as a lack of respect for boundaries or any tendencies towards manipulative behavior. It is also beneficial to be open about your past experiences with close, trusted friends or a counselor who can provide perspective and guidance as you navigate new relationships. Prioritize transparency and mutual respect, and choose partners and friends who encourage your independence and validate your feelings - a stark contrast to your past experiences.

Rebuilding your life after narcissism is a testament to your resilience and strength. It is not just about healing from the past but about creating a future that resonates with your newfound understanding of self-worth and independence. As you embark on this path, remember that each step, no matter how small, is a progression towards a more empowered and fulfilling life.

4.4 HEALING FROM NARCISSISTIC TRAUMA: THERAPY AND BEYOND

After stepping away from a relationship marked by narcissism, the remnants of manipulation and control can linger, manifesting as emotional triggers and deep-seated anxieties. To navigate through this complex aftermath, a multifaceted therapeutic approach is often necessary, integrating professional support with self-help strategies to foster recovery and promote long-term mental health.

Therapeutic Options

Cognitive-Behavioral Therapy (CBT) is among the most effective treatments for recovering from narcissistic abuse. This therapeutic model focuses on identifying and changing negative thought patterns and behaviors. By examining the ways in which narcissistic abuse has influenced your thoughts, CBT helps to reframe your internal dialogue to be more supportive and empowering. For instance, replacing thoughts like "I am not worthy" with "I am valuable, and my feelings matter" can significantly alter your emotional landscape and reduce feelings of worthlessness instilled by the narcissist.

Trauma-focused therapy is another pivotal approach beneficial, particularly for those who have experienced severe emotional or psychological trauma because of the relationship. This type of therapy delves into traumatic experiences, helping you process and make sense of what happened. This process is challenging, as it involves confronting painful memories and emotions. However, with the guidance of a skilled therapist, you can navigate this journey, gradually reducing the trauma's hold on your life and preventing long-term psychological consequences.

Group therapy offers unique benefits, particularly the invaluable feeling of not being alone in your experiences. Sharing your story with others who have faced similar challenges can validate your feelings and foster a sense of community and understanding. These sessions often provide perspective and coping strategies that might not have been considered before, allowing for a collective healing process where support is both given and received.

Self-Help Strategies

Complementing professional therapy with self-help strategies can enhance your recovery process. Mindfulness and meditation are powerful tools for managing stress and anxiety, common residuals of narcissistic abuse. These practices encourage a state of awareness and presence in the moment, helping to detach from harmful patterns of thought about past or future worries.

Regular meditation can lead to a profound sense of peace and inner stability, gradually diminishing the emotional turmoil left in the wake of the relationship.

Journaling is another effective self-help strategy that serves as both a therapeutic outlet and a means of tracking your healing progress. Writing down your thoughts and feelings daily can clarify your experiences and emotions, making it easier to process them. Furthermore, looking back on previous entries can offer insights into your personal growth over time, reinforcing the progress you have made and motivating continued efforts toward recovery.

Recognizing and Managing Triggers

Triggers - sudden reminders of the past that evoke intense emotional responses - can be particularly destabilizing for those recovering from narcissistic abuse. Identifying your triggers is a crucial step in managing them effectively. These can be specific phrases, places, or behaviors that transport you back to moments of abuse. Once identified, strategies such as grounding techniques - which involve focusing on physical sensations like touching a piece of fabric or focusing on your breath - can help to bring you back to the present moment, reducing the intensity of the emotional reaction.

Start by identifying the specific situations, events, or behaviors that trigger strong emotional reactions in you. Understanding your triggers can help you anticipate and prepare for them, as well as recognize patterns in your emotional responses.

Mindfulness techniques, such as deep breathing, grounding exercises, or meditation, can help you stay present and centered when you encounter emotional triggers. Mindfulness can help you observe your thoughts and emotions without judgment, allowing you to respond more consciously and skillfully.

Developing a routine for dealing with triggers when they arise is also essential. This might include planned responses, such as stepping away from a situation to practice breathing exercises or using affirmations to counteract negative thoughts triggered by the encounter. Over time, these responses can become automatic, significantly reducing the effects of triggers on your emotional well-being.

When you experience emotional triggers, negative thoughts and beliefs about yourself or others may arise. Challenge these thoughts by questioning their validity, considering alternative perspectives, or reframing them in a more positive and empowering way.

Be gentle and compassionate with yourself when you encounter emotional triggers. Remember that it is natural to have emotional reactions, and self-compassion can help you navigate difficult feelings with kindness and understanding.

Develop a safety plan that outlines coping strategies and support systems you can turn to when you experience emotional triggers. This plan may include self-soothing techniques, reaching out to trusted friends or professionals, or engaging in activities that help you feel calm and grounded.

If emotional triggers are significantly affecting your daily life or well-being, consider seeking support from a therapist, counselor, or mental health professional. Therapy can provide you with tools, techniques, and insights to better understand and cope with your triggers.

If your emotional triggers stem from past traumas, consider exploring trauma-focused therapy, such as EMDR (Eye Movement Desensitization and Reprocessing) or somatic experiencing. These modalities can help you process and heal from traumatic experiences in a safe and supportive environment.

Working with emotional triggers is a gradual and ongoing process that requires patience, self-awareness, and dedication to your healing journey. By implementing these strategies and seeking support when needed, you can effectively manage your triggers and cultivate greater emotional resilience and well-being.

Long-Term Mental Health Maintenance

Maintaining mental health after leaving a narcissistic relationship is an ongoing process that requires vigilance and commitment. Regular self-assessment is crucial to this process, as it helps identify any emerging patterns of negative thinking or behavior that may suggest a backslide into old, unhealthy habits. This might involve periodic check-ins with a therapist who can provide a professional perspective on your continued progress and help address any new challenges that arise even after formal therapy has ended.

Additionally, continued engagement in activities that promote mental health, such as regular exercise, sufficient sleep, and strong social connections, can support your overall well-being. These activities not only improve your physical health but also enhance your emotional resilience, providing a strong foundation for long-term recovery.

In essence, healing from narcissistic trauma is a dynamic and comprehensive process involving a combination of professional therapy, self-help strategies, and ongoing efforts to maintain mental health. Each element plays a crucial role in navigating the aftermath of the relationship, providing the tools and support necessary to rebuild a life defined not by manipulation and control but by resilience, recovery, and renewal.

The Importance of Support Networks in Recovery

In the aftermath of escaping a narcissistic relationship, the process of rebuilding your life can often feel like navigating a vast ocean with only the stars to guide you. In these moments, having a sturdy vessel in the form of a robust support network can make all the difference. Your support network acts not just as a safety net but as a powerful force that propels you forward, offering both emotional and practical assistance as you rebuild your independence and sense of self.

Building or rebuilding this network involves reaching out to friends, family, and professionals who understand and affirm your experiences. Initiating these connections might feel daunting, particularly if the relationship leads to a degree of isolation—a common tactic in narcissistic dynamics. Start with small steps, reach out to one person you trust, and gradually expand your circle. It is crucial to choose individuals who respect your boundaries and offer the kind of support that resonates with you, whether it is a listening ear, practical advice, or simply their presence that reminds you of your worth.

Professionals, particularly those experienced in dealing with the aftermath of abusive relationships, can provide critical insights and strategies tailored to your specific situation. Therapists, counselors, and support groups dedicated to survivors of narcissistic abuse can offer empathetic and empowering guidance. These professionals not only help you process your experiences but also equip you with tools to handle challenges and triggers as you move forward.

Utilizing Online and Community Resources

The digital age offers an expansive array of resources that can be particularly valuable when recovering from narcissistic abuse. Online forums and social media groups provide platforms where you can connect with others who have faced similar challenges. These spaces often foster a sense of community and understanding that can be incredibly affirming. You can share your experiences, learn from others, and receive encouragement in a way that is accessible from the safety of your home.

Community resources can also play a pivotal role. Local support groups, workshops, and seminars not only provide educational content but also offer opportunities to meet others in your community who share similar experiences. Engaging in these groups can help you feel less isolated and more connected to a supportive community. These interactions can be profoundly healing, as they reaffirm that you are not alone in your experiences and that recovery is indeed possible.

The Role of Mutual Support

Providing support to others who have endured similar trials can be unexpectedly therapeutic, reinforcing your recovery and understanding of the abuse you endured. Sharing your story and the strategies you have employed to overcome challenges can not only empower others but also reinforce your sense of self-efficacy. This mutual exchange of support can solidify your knowledge and emotional healing, contributing to a stronger sense of agency and purpose.

Participating in peer support activities, whether in informal settings like social media groups or more structured environments like support group meetings, can enhance your sense of community and connectedness. These roles allow you to give back, creating a positive feedback loop that bolsters your healing processes and those of others. The act of helping others can also provide a new perspective on your journey, highlighting the progress you have made and inspiring continued growth and resilience.

Setting Boundaries With Old Mutual Connections

Navigating relationships with your and your narcissistic partner's mutual acquaintances poses a unique challenge, particularly when these individuals may not fully understand or acknowledge your experiences. It is important to establish boundaries with these mutual connections to protect your emotional recovery. This might mean limiting the information you share about your recovery process or, in some cases, deciding to distance yourself from individuals who maintain a close relationship with the narcissist.

Communicating your needs clearly and assertively can help these acquaintances understand your perspective and respect your boundaries. It is okay to request that certain topics, such as details about the narcissist's life or your past relationship, are off-limits. If mutual connections are unable to respect these boundaries, it may be necessary to reevaluate these relationships and possibly reduce contact. It is not an act of hostility but a necessary measure to protect your mental health and ensure your recovery environment is supportive and safe.

In building and utilizing a support network, remember that the quality of connections often outweighs quantity. A few close, trustworthy relationships can provide immense support and facilitate a healthier, faster recovery. As you navigate this rebuilding phase, lean on your support network, value the mutual support you can offer and receive, and gradually establish a new life grounded in respect, understanding, and genuine connection.

4.5 FORGIVING NOT FORGETTING: MOVING FORWARD EMOTIONALLY

Forgiveness in the context of recovering from narcissistic abuse is an intricate and profoundly personal process. It does not imply a reconciliation or an acceptance of the narcissist's behavior, nor does it serve as an excuse for the harm he/she inflicted. Rather, forgiveness is about liberating yourself from the heavy chains of anger and resentment that can tie you to the past, hindering your ability to move forward and embrace a more peaceful, fulfilling future. It is about personal peace, a state where the actions of the narcissist no longer hold a controlling interest over your emotional well-being.

Understanding the role of forgiveness starts with acknowledging the hurt and recognizing that your feelings of betrayal and pain are valid. It is essential to process these emotions fully rather than suppress them, as unaddressed feelings can fester and lead to deeper emotional scars. Part of this process involves coming to terms with the reality of the narcissist's limitations—their inability to empathize with others or to possess genuine remorse. This acknowledgment does not minimize your experiences but places them in a context that can be understood and eventually accepted.

The act of forgiving a narcissist is not about condoning or forgetting the past. Instead, it is about making a conscious decision to release the grip that the residual anger and hurt have on your life. This does not mean the memories will vanish or the lessons learned will be discarded. On the contrary, remembering the lessons is crucial for protecting yourself in the future. It helps you recognize similar patterns in people or situations early on, enabling you to navigate away from potential harm before it unfolds.

Embarking on the steps towards forgiveness involves several stages, starting with the acknowledgment of the pain inflicted upon you. Writing a letter that you never send, detailing how the actions of the narcissist affected you, can be a therapeutic way to voice your feelings. Following this, try to express, even if just to yourself, an understanding of the narcissist's limitations. This understanding is not about empathy for the narcissist but about understanding the constraints of their character that prevent them from being a genuinely reciprocal partner. The final and perhaps the most challenging step is deciding to let go of the anger. This decision might not lead to immediate relief, but it sets the stage for gradual healing. Over time, the emotional charge of memories will start to fade, diminishing their power to affect your current emotional state.

Maintaining emotional safety as you forgive is paramount, especially as you navigate new relationships. Vigilance and boundaries are crucial, as they protect you from reverting to old patterns of interaction that left you vulnerable in the past. It involves actively choosing to engage in relationships with individuals who respect and honor your feelings and boundaries, who reciprocate your affection and respect, and who are consistent in their words and actions. This vigilance does not mean living in a state of perpetual suspicion but in a state of informed awareness, where past experiences are used to guide present decisions.

Forgiving a narcissist is ultimately an act of self-liberation. It frees you from the toxic ties to the past, allowing you to engage more fully and joyously with life. While the scars may remain, they no longer dictate your path nor dim the light of your future. As this chapter on forgiveness concludes, remember that each step forward in this process is a step towards reclaiming your peace and power. Here, you are not forgetting the past but choosing to no longer let it control your emotional landscape. This chapter sets the stage for exploring further dimensions of recovery, ensuring that as you move forward, you are equipped not only with resilience but also with a profound understanding of how to craft a life defined by your terms, values, and aspirations.

CHAPTER 5
SELF-DISCOVERY AND EMPOWERMENT

I magine emerging from a thick fog, where each step seemed more uncertain than the last, into a clearing where the sun finally begins to shine through. This is the essence of overcoming narcissistic abuse - a journey from darkness into light, where the rediscovery of your self-identity awaits. This chapter is dedicated to guiding you through this transformative process, helping you reclaim the parts of yourself that were overshadowed or suppressed during your time with a narcissist. Here, you will find tools and strategies to rebuild a stronger, more authentic you equipped with the understanding and skills to embrace life's pleasures and challenges with renewed confidence and clarity.

5.1 REDISCOVERING YOUR IDENTITY AFTER NARCISSISTIC ABUSE

Assessment of Past Influences

Your journey to reclaiming your identity begins with a critical assessment of how the narcissist influenced or suppressed it. Reflect on the aspects of yourself that you may have set aside to appease or accommodate the narcissist. Did you give up hobbies, career opportunities, or relationships? Did you alter your behavior, values, or aspirations? These questions are not meant to evoke regret but to help you understand the depth of the influence.

Engage in this reflective process through journal prompts designed to unearth these suppressed elements of your identity. For instance, write about a day spent entirely as you wish without considering anyone else's demands or expectations. What activities would you pursue? What values would guide your actions? This exercise is not just about imagining an ideal day but about reconnecting with your preferences and desires that were sidelined.

Creating a New Self-Concept

With a clearer understanding of the past, it is time to sculpt a new self-concept, one that resonates with who you are at your core, unencumbered by the narcissist's shadow.

Begin by listing your strengths - those you have always known and those you have discovered in adversity.

Recognize your resilience, your compassion, and your unique talents. Affirm these qualities daily to solidify your understanding of your worth.

Next, redefine your values and interests. Perhaps integrity, creativity, and community resonate with you. How do these values align with your current life? How can they guide your future? This alignment is the foundation of a robust self-concept that will guide your decisions and interactions, ensuring they reflect your true self.

Engaging in New Activities

Exploring new activities and hobbies is a powerful way to rein-force your newfound self-concept.

These pursuits are not just pastimes but pathways to self-discovery and expression.

Choose activities that align with your interests and values, whether that is learning a new art form, engaging in outdoor adventures, or volunteering in your community.

Each new activity is a step toward expanding your sense of self and your capabilities, reinforcing your independence and creativity.

Participation in these activities often leads to new social connec-tions with individuals who share your interests, providing a supportive community that celebrates your authentic self.

These relationships are built on mutual respect and common passions, offering a healthy contrast to the dynamics of your past narcissistic relationships.

Celebrating Small Victories

In the aftermath of narcissistic abuse, every step you take towards recovery and self-empowerment is a victory. Celebrate these accomplishments, no matter how small they may seem. Did you assert a boundary? Attend a new class on your own? Recognize a red flag? Each of these moments is a testament to your growth and resilience.

Celebrating these victories does more than boost your morale; it reinforces your progress and helps consolidate your new self-concept. Create a "victory log" where you record these achievements. Reviewing this log can be incredibly uplifting, especially on days when doubts or old patterns threaten to resurface. It serves as a tangible reminder of your journey and your capability to rebuild and renew your life on your terms.

Through these structured steps - reflecting on the past, redefining your self-concept, engaging in new activities, and celebrating your progress - you forge a path toward a fuller, more authentic existence. This process is not just about recovery but about discovery; not just about surviving but about thriving. As you continue to explore and reinforce your identity, you build a life defined not by your past but by your aspirations, values, and joys - a life in which you are passionately engaged, not just present.

5.2 ESTABLISHING HEALTHY RELATIONSHIPS: KNOWING WHAT TO LOOK FOR

When stepping into new relationships, especially after experiencing the complex dynamics of narcissistic abuse, it is crucial to arm yourself with the knowledge of healthy interaction as opposed to the one that raises alarms. This understanding not only safeguards you from potential emotional harm but also guides you in nurturing relationships that are genuinely supportive and fulfilling. Let us explore some essential aspects to help you navigate this new terrain.

Identifying red flags in potential relationships is your first line of defense against repeating past patterns. These warning signs often manifest subtly at first and can be easily overlooked if you are not vigilant. For instance, excessive charm can sometimes mask manipulative intentions, while swift intensities in affection, mirroring the love-bombing phase, can be a ploy to quickly engender your commitment. Another significant red flag is the disrespect of boundaries - pay attention to how well a person listens when you say no or express discomfort. Do they respect your wishes, or do they push and test limits, suggesting your boundaries are negotiable? Additionally, watch for signs of gaslighting - does the person twist words, situations, or your feelings, making you doubt your perception of reality? Being aware of these behaviors and acknowledging them as warning signs is crucial in preventing further emotional entanglement with potentially toxic individuals.

In contrast, the characteristics of healthy relationships include mutual respect, honesty, and supportive communication. These relationships are built on a foundation of trust, where each person feels safe to express their thoughts and feelings without fear of judgment or retaliation. In a healthy relationship, conflict is addressed constructively - without resorting to blame, shame, or avoidance. Each partner is viewed as an equal, with neither having to diminish themselves to make the other feel secure. Support in these relationships is not conditional; it does not fluctuate based on accomplishments or failures but is a steady presence offering reassurance and encouragement.

The pacing of new relationships is equally critical, particularly when moving past a history of abuse. After narcissistic relationships, where bonds are often formed and escalated rapidly to facilitate control, taking a slower approach can feel unfamiliar yet profoundly empowering. Allow relationships to evolve gradually. Enjoy the process of learning about each other over time rather than rushing into emotional commitments. This pacing helps build a solid foundation of friendship and trust, elements that are the bedrock of any lasting relationship. It also provides ample time for you to observe the person's behavior in various situations, offering insights into their character and compatibility with your life.

Past experiences with narcissism can help you make better relationship choices. Reflect on the dynamics that characterized your previous abusive relationship. Consider what made you vulnerable to such interactions and the signs you might have missed or ignored. Carry these reflections forward as learning tools, not as baggage. They are not there to cast a shadow over new opportunities but to serve as a guidepost, helping you navigate away from similar situations. For example, if you previously felt unheard or unseen, prioritize finding a partner who actively listens and shows genuine interest in your thoughts and life.

In this exploration of new relationships, remember that the goal is not just to avoid the negative but to foster and enjoy the positive. Healthy relationships are out there, and with the right tools and mindset, you are well-equipped to build connections that are not only safe but also enriching and joyous. Each step forward in this process reaffirms your growth, resilience, and deservedness of fulfilling relationships that respect and celebrate you for who you truly are.

5.3 THE POWER OF ASSERTIVENESS: LEARNING TO SAY NO

Assertiveness is an often misunderstood and underutilized skill, yet it is crucial in both personal and professional realms. At its core, assertiveness is about expressing your thoughts, feelings, and needs in a direct, honest, and appropriate way. It is about respecting yourself and others and navigating interactions without passivity or aggression. For those recovering from narcissistic abuse, mastering assertiveness is not just about improving communication; it is about reclaiming your voice and ensuring your needs are heard and respected. This empowerment plays a pivotal role in healing, as it directly counters the feelings of powerlessness and suppression experienced in manipulative relationships.

Practicing assertive communication is like strengthening a muscle; it requires consistent effort and strategy. One effective way to build this skill is through role-playing exercises that simulate challenging interactions. Imagine, for instance, a scenario where you need to refuse an unreasonable request from a colleague. How would you articulate your refusal clearly and respectfully? Role-playing this situation with a friend or therapist can provide a safe space to experiment with different responses and receive feedback. This practice helps refine your ability to maintain your ground respectfully and effectively, which is crucial for interactions with both narcissists and others who may take advantage of non-assertive behavior.

Another exercise is the "assertiveness script" practice. It involves preparing a concise script that outlines how to express a difficult message. For example, if you need to set a boundary with someone, your script might start with an "I" statement that focuses on your feelings rather than blaming the other person: "I feel overwhelmed when I have too many tasks on my plate. I need to focus on my current projects before taking on new ones." This method not only clarifies your message but also prepares you to deliver it with confidence and clarity.

Handling pushback or resistance is perhaps the most challenging aspect of being assertive, especially for those accustomed to yielding to others' demands to avoid conflict. When you first start asserting yourself, you might encounter resistance, which can manifest as guilt-tripping, anger, or even mockery. Preparing for these reactions and developing strategies to maintain your stance is crucial. One effective approach is the broken record technique. This approach involves calmly and persistently repeating your point without getting drawn into an argument or sidetracked by the other person's reactions. For example, if someone continues to pressure you to take on extra work, keep reiterating, "I understand your need for help, but as I mentioned, I cannot commit to more tasks at the moment."

Furthermore, assertiveness should be viewed not just as a communication tool but as a form of self-care. Being assertive protects your mental health by preventing resentment, reducing stress, and building self-confidence. Every time you assert yourself, you affirm your values, your rights, and your needs. Such an assertion is a powerful reminder that you are worthy of respect and that your needs matter just as much as anyone else's. It can be particularly healing for those who have been in relationships where their needs were consistently sidelined or ignored.

Incorporating assertiveness into your daily life involves continuous practice and dedication. Start with small, manageable situations where the stakes are not too high, and gradually work your way up to more challenging scenarios. Celebrate your successes along the way, and be patient with yourself during setbacks. Remember, the goal is not perfection but progress. Each step forward in asserting yourself rebuilds your self-esteem and reinforces your independence, essential components of your journey toward recovery and empowerment.

5.4 RECLAIMING YOUR EMOTIONAL AUTONOMY

Emotional autonomy is a vital aspect of personal growth and recovery, particularly for those healing from narcissistic abuse. It represents your ability to maintain your emotional health, make decisions based on your needs and feelings, and not be overly influenced or controlled by others' emotions. For individuals coming out of relationships with blurred or nonexistent emotional boundaries, establishing emotional autonomy is both liberating and essential. It marks the shift from a state where your emotional well-being was tied to the whims and moods of a narcissist to a position of self-empowerment and independence.

The first step towards reclaiming this autonomy involves disconnecting from the emotional dependencies that may have formed during the relationship with the narcissist. These dependencies often develop as mechanisms to cope with the unpredictability and manipulation inherent in such relationships. However, they can leave you vulnerable to external emotional influences even after the relationship has ended. To begin disconnecting, it is crucial to recognize these dependencies. Reflect on moments when your partner's actions or approval influenced your mood and decisions. Awareness is the precursor to change, and simply by acknowledging these patterns, you start the process of untangling yourself from them.

One effective strategy for severing these ties is to start defining and asserting your emotional needs. This might mean setting aside time for activities that fulfill you personally, whether that's spending time alone, engaging with art, or spending time in nature. It could also involve seeking out new relationships and communities that support reciprocal emotional exchange rather than one-sided emotional labor. Gradually, as you prioritize your needs and engage in fulfilling activities, you diminish the emotional hold the narcissist had, replacing it with a self-sufficient and gratifying emotional life.

Developing emotional self-sufficiency is another critical component of reclaiming your autonomy. It involves cultivating the ability to manage your emotions internally rather than relying on external validation or guidance. Techniques such as mindfulness meditation can be incredibly beneficial here. Mindfulness encourages you to observe your thoughts and feelings without judgment, fostering a deep, internal understanding of your emotional landscape. This practice can help you recognize emotional triggers and patterns, equipping you with the knowledge to manage them proactively.

Another technique involves emotional regulation exercises. These are strategies used to manage and modify intense emotions in healthy ways. For instance, if you feel overwhelmed, techniques such as deep breathing, progressive muscle relaxation, or grounding exercises can help restore a sense of calm. Over time, these practices not only enhance your ability to handle emotions independently but also strengthen your overall emotional resilience, making you less susceptible to external emotional pressures.

Maintaining emotional boundaries is the final, ongoing part of reclaiming your emotional autonomy. These boundaries are the limits you set on how much you allow others to affect your emotions and how you respond to the emotions of others. Establishing clear boundaries involves communicating your emotional needs and limits to others and adhering to them, even when pressured to do otherwise. For example, if you decide that you will not engage in conversations that put down your achievements or feelings, you must be prepared to assertively end such discussions or remove yourself from situations where this boundary is not respected.

It is also crucial to be mindful of not just setting boundaries but respecting them consistently. This consistency sends a clear message to others about your expectations and helps prevent old patterns from reemerging. Additionally, be prepared to reevaluate and adjust your boundaries as needed. As you grow and your situation changes, your emotional needs might also shift.

Regularly reflecting on and adjusting your boundaries ensures they continue to serve your best interests and support your emotional autonomy.

In fostering your emotional autonomy, you empower yourself to live a life defined not by past abuses or external validations but by your values, choices, and emotional integrity. This shift is not just about overcoming the past but about building a foundation for a fulfilling and emotionally healthy future. As you implement these strategies and strengthen your emotional autonomy, you increasingly become the architect of your emotional well-being, capable of navigating life's challenges with resilience and self-assurance.

Building Resilience: Lessons from Survivors

Resilience is often likened to the strength and flexibility of bamboo; it bends but does not break. In the context of surviving narcissistic abuse, resilience is that profound strength that allows individuals not just to survive but to thrive, transforming painful experiences into pillars of growth and renewal. The stories of those who have walked this path before you can serve as powerful testimonies to the resilience of the human spirit. Consider the story of Clara, a former victim of narcissistic abuse who reclaimed her life through sheer resilience. One day, I will tell my own story, and believe me, you will be surprised. After years of manipulation and an emotional rollercoaster, I finally found my way to peace and calm. The journey was fraught with challenges, including financial hardship, self-doubt, and isolation. However, through each obstacle, I learned to harness my inner strength and resilience, gradually regaining control over my life piece by piece. Today, I am driven by a desire to help others who are facing similar struggles. My story is a testament to the fact that while the path to recovery can be arduous, it is also filled with opportunities for personal transformation and empowerment.

Key strategies that helped me and many others rebuild their lives can be instrumental for anyone emerging from the shadows of narcissistic abuse. One such strategy is the development of adaptive coping mechanisms. These are personalized techniques that individuals create to manage stress and emotional pain in healthier ways. For me, this involved engaging in a deep educational process of learning about the NPD phenomenon. This knowledge helped me stay grounded and cope effectively with overwhelming stress. Another effective coping mechanism can be structured journaling, where you not only express your thoughts and emotions but also describe the facts and track your progress and setbacks. This practice can help you recall all the episodes that happened to you once you have another emotional setback. Through this process, you can also gain insights into your emotional triggers and patterns, providing a clearer perspective on your journey and allowing you to make more informed decisions about your path forward.

Building a strong support network is another cornerstone of resilience. This network should include individuals who are empathetic and supportive, providing a safe space for you to express your feelings and experiences. For many survivors, finding support groups, either online or in the community where members share similar experiences, can be particularly beneficial. These groups offer a sense of belonging and understanding that can be hard to find elsewhere. Additionally, professional support from therapists or counselors trained in dealing with emotional abuse can provide guidance and tools to manage the complex emotions that arise from such experiences. This professional input is crucial, especially in navigating the intense feelings of guilt, shame, or anger that often accompany the aftermath of narcissistic abuse.

Incorporating resilience-building practices into daily life is essential for maintaining and strengthening your psychological and emotional well-being. Setting realistic goals is a practical approach to building resilience. Start with small, achievable goals that help boost your confidence and sense of accomplishment. For instance, it might be as simple as committing to a daily walk or cooking a healthy meal for yourself. Each small victory contributes to a larger sense of self-efficacy and independence. Practicing gratitude is another resilience-enhancing practice. By focusing on what you are thankful for, you shift your perspective from what you have lost to what you still have and what is possible. This shift can significantly improve your mood and outlook on life, providing a buffer against despair and negativity.

Regular physical activity is also a powerful tool for building resilience. Exercise not only improves your physical health but also profoundly affects your mental health. It releases endorphins, the body's natural mood lifters, and helps reduce symptoms of anxiety and depression. Whether it is yoga, running, or dancing, find a physical activity that you enjoy and make it a part of your routine. The discipline and focus required when engaging in physical exercise can also help divert your mind from dwelling on the past, channeling your energy into positive and healthful pursuits.

Lastly, learning from setbacks rather than viewing them as failures is crucial for developing a resilient mindset. Setbacks are inevitable, whether they are emotional relapses, relationship difficulties, or other life stressors. However, each setback provides valuable insights into strategies that work and those that do not, helping you better prepare for future challenges. When faced with a setback, take the time to analyze what happened and why. What can you learn from this experience? How can you adjust your strategies to better cope with similar situations in the future? This reflective approach turns potential stumbling blocks into stepping stones, fostering a resilience that not only sustains you through recovery but also empowers you to embrace and overcome future challenges.

By embracing these resilience-building strategies and learning from those who have successfully navigated their way out of narcissistic abuse, you equip yourself with the tools and perspectives necessary to not just recover but to thrive. Each step you take on this path reinforces your strength, your worth, and your capacity to transform challenges into catalysts for growth and renewal.

5.5 ADOPTING THE GRAY ROCK METHOD: BECOMING EMOTIONALLY UNINTERESTING TO NARCISSISTS

In navigating the turbulent waters left in the wake of narcissistic relationships, the Gray Rock Method emerges as a strategic beacon, guiding those ensnared by narcissistic allure towards calmer, less reactive interactions. This method, predicated on the principle of emotional disengagement, involves making oneself as uninteresting as a gray rock. The rationale is straightforward yet profound: narcissists thrive on the emotional response of others, and by denying them this, you reduce their interest and, consequently, their manipulative interactions.

The Gray Rock Method is not about changing who you are but rather how you respond in the presence of a narcissist. It is a performance of sorts, one where you present yourself as utterly unremarkable, offering no emotional feedback that might fuel the narcissist's need for drama and attention. For instance, when a narcissist attempts to provoke you with a barbed comment or an unreasonable request, instead of reacting with anger or defense, you might respond with evasive answers like "Hmm," "I see," or "That is interesting." These phrases are deliberately mundane and provide no foothold for escalation.

Implementing this method requires consistent practice and mindfulness, especially if your natural inclination is to engage or confront. Begin by identifying scenarios where you typically experience heightened emotional interactions with the narcissist. Plan your responses ahead of these encounters, rehearsing neutral statements and keeping your tone as flat as possible. It is crucial to monitor not just what you say but also your nonverbal cues. Maintain minimal eye contact, limit gestures, and keep your facial expressions neutral. Over time, these responses will become more natural, effectively making you a less appealing target for narcissistic engagement.

While the benefits of the Gray Rock Method, particularly its ability to avoid escalation and reduce emotional drain, are significant, it is important to acknowledge its limitations. This strategy is particularly effective in situations where you must maintain contact with a narcissist, perhaps due to co-parenting or workplace connections, but it is not a holistic solution for deeper emotional or physical abuse. When your safety and well-being are at risk, more definitive actions, such as severing ties or seeking professional intervention, may be necessary.

Moreover, the long-term implications of employing the Gray Rock Method warrant consideration. Consistently muting your emotional expressions can feel alienating and can sometimes lead to a disconnection from your feelings. It is essential, therefore, to have outlets in your life where you can express yourself openly and authentically. Ensure that you maintain strong, supportive relationships with friends or family members, engage in hobbies that bring you joy, and possibly seek therapy to process your emotions safely and constructively.

As you utilize the Gray Rock Method, remember that it is a tool, not a transformation. It is a means to navigate specific interactions without letting them deplete you emotionally. By mastering this method, you enhance your ability to dictate the terms of engagement with the narcissist, preserving your emotional energy for the relationships and activities that truly matter.

As this chapter closes, we reflect on the Gray Rock Method not just as a strategy for dealing with narcissists but as part of a broader toolkit for anyone seeking to reclaim their life from the shadows of manipulation. It stands alongside assertiveness, emotional autonomy, and resilience-building as essential techniques for those journeying toward recovery and empowerment. As we turn the page, we continue to explore additional strategies that support this journey, ensuring that each step taken is grounded in understanding, strength, and a renewed sense of self.

CHAPTER 6
ADVANCED COPING STRATEGIES

In the labyrinth of narcissistic relationships, navigating the complex interplay of manipulation and emotional upheaval can often feel overwhelming.

However, when children are caught in the crossfire, the stakes become significantly higher, demanding not just resilience but a strategic approach to safeguarding their emotional and psychological well-being. This chapter delves into the nuanced challenges of co-parenting with a narcissist, offering you a compass to steer through these turbulent waters with grace and efficacy.

6.1 CO-PARENTING WITH A NARCISSIST: PROTECTING YOUR CHILDREN AND YOURSELF

In the shadows of a relationship marred by narcissism, the paramount concern shifts swiftly to the innocence caught in its wake - the children. Co-parenting under such circumstances requires a deft balance of firmness and tact as you navigate not only your well-being but also that of your children, ensuring they emerge from this ordeal unscathed and resilient.

Establishing Legal Boundaries

Navigating the legalities of co-parenting with a narcissist necessitates a clear and strategic approach to shield your children from the potential volatility of the narcissist's behaviors. Collaborating with legal professionals who are well-versed in handling high-conflict custody cases becomes indispensable. These experts can guide you in establishing custody arrangements that prioritize the children's safety and emotional health. For instance, specifying the terms of visitation and custody right down to the exchange locations can mitigate unnecessary friction. Additionally, legal stipulations can be crafted to limit the narcissist's ability to make unilateral decisions that might affect the children adversely. The goal here is to create a structured legal framework that minimizes the narcissist's opportunities for manipulation and control, effectively placing a safety net around the emotional and physical well-being of your children.

Communication Strategies

When it comes to communicating with a narcissistic ex-partner, less is more. Reducing direct contact can significantly lower the chances of conflicts and manipulative exchanges. Employing written forms of communication, such as emails or text messages, provides a clear record of interactions and agreements, which can be invaluable in disputes. Furthermore, using third-party communication services designed for divorced or separated parents can streamline interactions, focusing solely on the logistics of co-parenting rather than personal conflicts. These platforms can help maintain a professional tone in all communications, keeping exchanges brief, factual, and devoid of emotional content, thus depriving the narcissist of the emotional reactions they often seek.

Shielding Children from Conflict

Protecting your children from the emotional turbulence of parental conflict involves more than just physical separation from arguments. It extends into the realms of emotional shielding and education. Explaining the dynamics of the conflicts neutrally, without demonizing the narcissistic parent, is crucial. This approach fosters an environment of openness, allowing children to express their feelings and concerns without fear of retribution or guilt. For example, explaining that "sometimes adults disagree, and it is okay to agree to disagree" helps children understand conflict without feeling compelled to choose sides.

Supporting Children's Emotional Needs

Amidst the complexities of co-parenting with a narcissist, logistical and legal challenges can sometimes overshadow your children's emotional needs. Actively supporting and validating their feelings is crucial. Engage in regular, open conversations with your children, allowing them to express their thoughts and emotions about their experiences with the narcissistic parent without judgment. Recognize signs of emotional manipulation, such as confusion, anxiety, or guilt, stemming from interactions with the narcissistic parent, and address these promptly with the help of a child psychologist if necessary. Providing a stable, loving environment where the children feel secure and valued helps counterbalance the instability they may experience in their interactions with the narcissistic parent. This support not only aids in their immediate emotional resilience but also lays the foundation for healthy emotional relationships in the future.

In fostering a co-parenting environment that prioritizes the well-being of your children, you advocate not just for your peace but for the future resilience and emotional health of your children. This strategic approach to co-parenting allows you to mitigate the challenges posed by the narcissist's behavior, ensuring that your children have the stable, supportive foundation they need to thrive.

6.2 WHEN NARCISSISM MEETS TECHNOLOGY: DIGITAL BOUNDARIES AND SAFETY

In today's interconnected world, technology offers unprecedented convenience and connectivity. However, it also provides a fertile playground for narcissists to extend their influence and control far beyond personal interactions.

Understanding how narcissists can manipulate digital tools is crucial for protecting yourself and maintaining your autonomy in the digital space.

Narcissists use various aspects of digital communication, such as social media, texting, and email, to manipulate and control their targets. This manipulation can range from constant monitoring of your emails and phone to commenting on your social media posts.

For instance, a narcissist might use social media to track your movements and interactions, commenting or messaging in ways that may initially seem caring but are actually meant to control or induce guilt.

Setting digital boundaries is, therefore, not just advisable; it is necessary. Start by auditing your digital footprints. Review your social media accounts and consider changes to your privacy settings to control who can see your posts, who can tag you, and who can comment on your activities. It might also be beneficial not to reveal all your social accounts and activities.

Additionally, consider taking periodic digital detoxes, stepping away from online platforms that might serve as venues for your narcissist to control you.

This not only gives you a break from potential drama but also helps reinforce your boundaries, making it clear that you are in control of your life.

Dealing with a narcissist requires a proactive approach. It is advisable to use strong, unique passwords for all your accounts and enable two-factor authentication, when available, to protect your accounts from being hacked by the narcissist, who may attempt to gather information about what you are doing and who you are communicating with.

Using anonymous accounts or pseudonyms for certain online activities can also be a wise move, especially in forums or groups where you discuss sensitive issues like narcissistic abuse.

Keeping your main accounts private and having separate ones for public engagement can help maintain a healthy distance between your personal life and your online persona.

Navigating the digital world while dealing with a narcissist can indeed be challenging, but with the right strategies and precautions, you can maintain your digital autonomy and safety.

By understanding the tactics employed by narcissists in digital spaces, setting firm boundaries, actively protecting your online presence, and knowing how to handle harassment, you empower yourself to use technology on your terms, free from manipulation and control.

6.3 LEGAL TACTICS AND RIGHTS AGAINST NARCISSISTIC ABUSE

Navigating the legal landscape when confronted with narcissistic abuse necessitates a foundational understanding of your rights, which serve as your armor and shield in such tumultuous circumstances. Knowing these rights intimately empowers you to stand firmly grounded, even as the storm of manipulation and deceit tries to sweep you off your feet. Your fundamental legal rights - including the right to privacy, safety, and freedom from harassment - are enshrined in laws designed to protect individuals from undue harm, both physical and emotional.

First, the right to privacy underpins your ability to shield personal information and interactions from unwarranted intrusion by a narcissist. This right is crucial in preventing a narcissist from invading your personal space or accessing information that could be used for manipulation or retaliation. Understanding this right can help you secure your communications, reinforce social media privacy settings, and safeguard personal records. Additionally, the right to safety is a cornerstone of legal protection against physical and psychological harm. It encompasses the right to secure yourself and your dependents from threats or actions that compromise your well-being. In the context of narcissistic abuse, this could translate into obtaining restraining orders or protective orders that legally mandate the narcissist to maintain a distance or cease certain behaviors.

Moreover, the right to be free from harassment is particularly pertinent. Harassment in this scenario might manifest through relentless calls, messages, stalking, or public defamation—all tactics commonly employed by narcissists to intimidate and control their targets. Legal statutes provide mechanisms through which such harassment can be reported and curtailed. Familiarizing yourself with these provisions can equip you with the tools to initiate legal action when the boundaries of acceptable behavior are crossed, thereby offering a form of recourse that can significantly alleviate the coercive pressure exerted by a narcissist.

The effective use of the legal system as a means of protection requires more than just a passive awareness of these rights; it demands active engagement and strategic action. For those facing the daunting prospect of legal confrontation with a narcissist, the first step often involves securing a restraining order or other legal injunctions that provide immediate relief from imminent threats. These legal tools are designed to create a buffer between you and the narcissist, enforcing a boundary that is legally recognized and punishable if violated. Understanding the criteria and process for obtaining these protections is crucial. It typically involves presenting evidence of the abuse, which underscores the importance of documentation - a meticulous record of incidents that can substantiate your claims.

Documenting abuse for legal purposes is a meticulous and strategic process that involves more than just keeping a diary of events. It is about creating a comprehensive and factual account of interactions that can serve as evidence in legal proceedings. This step might include saving texts, emails, voicemails, and other communications that demonstrate the narcissist's abusive patterns or threats. Photographic evidence of physical abuse or property damage, corroborated by medical or police records, can also be pivotal. Additionally, maintaining a log of incidents that includes dates, times, and detailed descriptions of interactions can help illustrate the ongoing nature and effects of the abuse, providing a timeline that can be critical in legal contexts.

Choosing the right legal support is perhaps one of the most critical decisions in this journey. Not all attorneys are familiar with the nuances of narcissistic abuse, which can sometimes be subtle and psychologically complex. Finding a legal advisor who understands the dynamics of such abuse and is experienced in handling similar cases can make a significant difference in the outcome of your legal endeavors. Look for professionals who specialize in domestic abuse or psychological manipulation and come prepared with recommendations from trusted sources or positive testimonials. The right legal counsel not only offers expert guidance through the complexities of the legal process but also provides the emotional reassurance that comes from being understood and supported.

In navigating these legal avenues, you arm yourself with the knowledge and power to reclaim control over your life and ensure your safety and dignity. The legal system, with its rights and protections, serves as a crucial ally in the battle against narcissistic abuse, offering pathways to security and recovery for those who are brave enough to pursue them.

6.4 ADVANCED SELF-CARE: PSYCHOLOGICAL AND SPIRITUAL PRACTICES FOR RECOVERY

In the aftermath of navigating life with a narcissist, it is not just about moving forward; it is about moving forward with intention and care. Advanced psychological techniques and spiritual practices offer profound tools for healing. Engaging in these practices can help you manage the emotional residue of past abuse and cultivate a resilient, enlightened self.

Integrating Advanced Psychological Techniques

The journey toward recovery often necessitates more than traditional therapy; it requires techniques that empower you to reshape your narrative and embrace a future unchained from past traumas. Cognitive reframing and Acceptance and Commitment Therapy (ACT) are two such transformative approaches. Cognitive reframing involves identifying and changing your thought patterns to disrupt the negative mental frameworks that a narcissistic relationship might have imprinted on you. For instance, if you find yourself contemplating over a belief that you are unworthy of respect because of the narcissist's past demeaning treatments, cognitive reframing helps you challenge and alter these thoughts. It encourages you to replace them with more balanced and self-affirming perspectives that help you recognize your inherent worth independent of external validation.

ACT, on the other hand, introduces you to mindfulness-based strategies that encourage you to accept your thoughts and feelings rather than fighting or feeling ashamed of them. This acceptance is paired with commitment to actions that align with your values, creating a life enriched by purpose and clarity. For someone emerging from the shadow of narcissistic abuse, ACT provides the tools to acknowledge painful feelings without letting them dictate your actions, enabling you to commit to living according to your chosen values, such as trust, compassion, and resilience.

Spiritual Healing Practices

Spirituality, whether tied to a specific religion or more personal interpretations of connection and purpose, can play a critical role in healing from narcissistic abuse. Practices like meditation, guided imagery, and spiritual retreats serve not only as sources of solace but also as platforms for profound self-discovery and recovery. Meditation can help you develop a heightened awareness of your inner state and a deeper sense of peace to alleviate the anxiety and stress that often linger after toxic relationships. Guided imagery enhances this process by inviting you to visualize a place where you feel safe and loved, reinforcing feelings of security and self-worth.

Participating in spiritual retreats can also offer new perspectives and supportive communities that nurture your healing process. These retreats provide a space to disconnect from daily stressors and connect with others who share similar experiences and aspirations, facilitating a collective journey of healing and growth. The focus on spiritual well-being helps reframe your experiences, enabling you to draw strength from your inner self and the community around you, fostering resilience against future emotional disruptions.

Routine and Ritual in Recovery

Establishing routine or personal rituals can be incredibly grounding in the chaotic aftermath of narcissistic abuse. These routines do not have to be rigid or overwhelming; rather, they should include activities that promote stability and emotional health. Incorporating simple practices, such as morning walks, journaling, or regular meetups with supportive friends, can immensely enhance your daily well-being. Rituals might include more personalized practices, like evening gratitude reflections or weekly attendance at a community class that aligns with your interests or spiritual beliefs. These activities provide anchors, reducing unpredictability and giving your days structure and purpose, which is beneficial especially in times of emotional turmoil.

Continued Growth and Education

Your path to recovery is bolstered by ongoing personal growth and education. Understanding the psychological underpinnings of narcissistic behaviors and recognizing their effects on relationships empowers you to navigate future interactions more wisely. Engaging in workshops, reading relevant literature, and participating in discussions about narcissism and psychological health can deepen your understanding and equip you with the knowledge to protect yourself from similar situations in the future. This continuous learning process nurtures your intellectual curiosity and reinforces your emotional defenses, enabling you to foster relationships that are healthy, respectful, and enriching.

In embracing these advanced coping strategies, you forge a path defined not by past abuses but by your resilience and capacity for growth. The psychological and spiritual practices outlined here offer a blueprint for thriving rather than just simply surviving, turning the lessons learned from painful experiences into steppingstones for a fulfilled and purposeful life.

As this chapter concludes, remember the power of advanced self-care techniques in your healing journey. From the psychological reshaping offered by cognitive refraining and ACT to the profound peace found in spiritual practices, these strategies are vital tools in your recovery arsenal. They provide the strength and stability needed to navigate post-narcissistic life, ensuring that each step forward is taken with intention and hope. Moving into the next chapter, we will explore the broader societal implications of narcissistic behaviors to give you the knowledge needed to advocate for change, both personally and within your wider community.

CONCLUSION

If you have made it to this page, congratulations on taking this journey! I hope you feel more prepared, informed, and fully equipped to move forward. You have now learned how to regain control over your life, and know exactly what you need to do to protect your mental health and well-being.

My deepest wish is that the knowledge you gain here serves as a foundation in your pursuit of happiness. Remember —KNOWLEDGE is POWER.

As I mentioned before, journaling is an especially valuable tool for emotional self-care. It helps you to articulate your thoughts and feelings more effectively, reflect on your experiences, and gain clarity. Moreover, it helps you recall the FACTS from your previous experience with a narcissist. And perhaps, if they come back into your life—or you feel tempted to contact them—you can revisit your journal entries and make the right decision.

About the Author

As a gallerist, author, advocate for women's rights, an active member of the National Association of Women Business Owners (NAWBO), the National Organization for Women (NOW), and the Women's Chamber of Commerce of Palm Beach, Gulbrandsen collaborates with like-minded individuals to drive positive change and create opportunities in business and society.

Gulbrandsen's books serve as a platform to inspire and empower both men and women to break barriers and pursue their dreams fearlessly. Her latest release, *"Sleeping with a Narcissist"*, focuses on the complexities of narcissistic relationships, and their often-over-looked impact on mental health and well-being.

With a deep commitment to helping individuals navigate the challenges posed by narcissism, Gulbrandsen aims to provide readers with a comprehensive understanding of manipulative tactics, offering insights and practical strategies for breaking through, healing, and empowerment.

"The mission of this book is to empower those affected by narcissistic relationships and guide them towards clarity and support. I believe in the power of education and awareness to help individuals reclaim their lives and build healthier relationships. By sharing knowledge and personal stories, I hope to inspire resilience and foster healing."

LIUBOV GULBRANDSEN